KNOW YOUR DOG

KNOW YOUR DOG

AN OWNER'S GUIDE TO DOG BEHAVIOR

DR. BRUCE FOGLE

Photography by David Ward
Additional photography Jane Burton

DORLING KINDERSLEY
LONDON • NEW YORK • STUTTGART

A DORLING KINDERSLEY BOOK

Project Editor Candida Ross-Macdonald
Art Editor Nigel Hazle
Managing Editor Krystyna Mayer
Managing Art Editor Derek Coombes
Production Manager Maryann Rogers
U.S. Editor Mary Ann Lynch

First American Edition, 1992
10 9 8 7 6 5 4 3 2

Published in the United States by
Dorling Kindersley, Inc., 95 Madison Avenue,
New York, New York 10016

Library of Congress Cataloging-in-Publication Data
Fogle, Bruce
    Know your dog : an owner's guide to dog behavior / Bruce Fogle.
        p.   cm.
    Includes index.
    ISBN 1–56458–080–6
    1. Dogs—Behavior.   I. Title.
SF433.F65   1992
636.7'0887—dc20   92–4497
                                                              CIP

Originated by Colourscan, Singapore
Printed and bound by Mondadori, Italy

CONTENTS

THE WOLF AT THE DOOR

IT COMES AS no surprise to those of us who share our homes with dogs that their species, *Canis familiaris*, is in many ways much like ours. We are both predators, surviving by preying upon other animals. Both of us are social animals that enjoy the companionship of others of our own species, and pack animals to the very depths of our being. We work well together and, for better or worse, are most contented either when we have leaders to follow and respect, or when we become leaders ourselves. Our two species have a diverse range of emotions and can feel jealousy, affection, anger, or tolerance toward others of their kind. Our needs are so similar that, of all the animal species that ever evolved, the dog was the first to be invited into our homes. It is due to its behavioral characteristics, as well as its usefulness, that the dog has become "man's best friend."

One of a crowd
Although their appearances and temperaments vary, all of these dogs are pack animals, needing social contact to thrive.

Appealing
We have created some breeds that particularly appeal to us, like the Australian Silky Terrier.

Dogs accompanied us from primitive campsites to agricultural settlements and even to the massive cities in which we live today. They made these transitions so successfully because they are highly effective at adapting to changing conditions. A dramatically wide range of shapes and sizes helped them through these transitions, but it is their varied natures that have made dogs the most popular pet in the world today.

With help from us, dogs have evolved different characteristics to help them survive the varying environments in which we place them. Today, there are over 400 recognized breeds of dogs worldwide. These breeds exist at our whim. We create new breeds and combine or lose old ones completely according to our needs or the dictates of fashion. Because of this, it is sometimes argued that dogs are an unnatural and warped product of mankind's intervention.

Survival tactics
The intelligence and curiosity of the natural dog enabled it to adapt to varying circumstances.

Versatility
Originally bred as working dogs, Newfoundlands are now kept as family pets, showing the adaptability typical of the dog.

Waiting for the cue
No matter what their breed, dogs see humans as large canines, and look to us for leadership.

All breeds of dog are the product of artificial rather than natural selection. Even the Australian dingo and the Papua New Guinea singing dog, which mate without the pressure of human selection, are the result of our intervention, because thousands of years ago humans introduced domesticated dogs to those locations. All of our canine companions today are the result of the practical, aesthetic, economic, or even ritual needs of preceding human generations. Some dogs are independent, while others have been bred to be more trainable or obedient.

Raising the alarm
The dog's bark has been encouraged through selective breeding, because it suits us to have vocal guard dogs.

We sometimes confuse what suits us in a dog's behavior with what is naturally best for the dog itself, making the mistake of thinking that the more trainable a dog is, the more intelligent it is. In fact, the intractable stray dog that survives by its own wits might be more intelligent than the dog who jumps through hoops at its owner's command. My retrievers, lying on the floor by my side, are not the result of natural survival of the fittest. Although they are large and strong, they would be too gentle to survive for long in the wild.

Family features
Many of the larger spitz-type breeds retain a physical as well as a mental similarity to their wolf ancestors.

In spite of all our intervention, however, elements of the dog's ancestry can still be seen in our pets. Even in those breeds that are the most dramatically different from their wolf roots – tiny breeds, such as the Pekingese or Chihuahua, or delicate-looking dogs like the Italian Greyhound – the bedrock of their original wild behavior survives. They still think like pack

All sorts
All of these dogs share common thought and behavior patterns. To satisfy our needs, we have accentuated certain traits in some breeds and diminished them in others.

8

animals. They still have the senses of a hunter. They court, mate, and raise their young in the same way as other independent canine species such as the wolf.

These facets of our companions are often overlooked. Because we share so many needs, emotions, and patterns of behavior with dogs, and because we have been influencing their characters for thousands of years, it is easier for us to think like them than like any other domesticated species. But we must remember that, although we share our homes with dogs, they differ from us in many ways.

Born fighting
Some dogs have been bred as fighting dogs for sport. If we keep these breeds, we must understand what motivates them.

In order to know your dog completely, it is vital to understand that, just as we sometimes think of our canine companions as humans in strange disguises, they think of us as rather odd dogs. We might be bigger than them, we certainly smell different, and we are able to do awesome things like use can openers, but they can still only think of us as other dogs and treat us accordingly. Their relationships with us are all based on this fact. To the core of its being, even the smallest and fluffiest dog will always remain true to its roots, a wolf in disguise.

THE PACK INSTINCT

Paying respect
This West Highland White Terrier shows submissive behavior by jumping up to lick the Italian Spinone's mouth. Dogs show similar submissive feelings when they try to lick our faces.

THE PACK MENTALITY of hunting, resting, eating, and sleeping together is what has made dogs so successful as a species. This mentality comes from their wolf forebears. Throughout the Northern Hemisphere, wolves radiated out after the last Ice Age, following the herds of large, hoofed animals that were their prey. We humans did the same, the only other social species to migrate north at that time. Young wolves were captured, raised, and played with by our ancestors, who selected which individuals they would eat, and which they would allow to breed.

Two's company
Having sensed something, these two Miniature Schnauzers concentrate intently. A natural pack contains a leader and several followers, but it only takes two to make a dog pack.

Choosing a leader
These Yorkshire Terriers gather around someone they have never met, knowing from experience that humans are excellent pack leaders.

Just as in the wild, superior size and mental acuity decided who would lead in the pack hierarchy of the dogs that evolved as a result of this human selection. In both situations, males usually dominate because of physical strength. Ritual threats, such as growling and showing the teeth,

prevent serious fights and maintain rank and hierarchy. Dogs first learn these rituals and find their place in the pack during play as puppies. Rough-and-tumbles become rougher as the puppies mature, leading to disputes that are won by the strongest in body and spirit. Eventually the most dominant dog emerges, asserting his authority through his body language. Other pack members are usually content to submit to their leader, and indicate this through their own gestures and expressions, although eventually a spirited younger male will challenge the leader's authority.

Team practice
These Norwegian Buhunds naturally coordinate their activities, like the packs of wolves from which they evolved. Resting, waking, and being active together enables them to work as a team.

Other behavior patterns that we see in our domestic dogs are also remnants of this wolf-pack mentality. A canine pack needs a territory in which to hunt and rest. It marks out this territory with body wastes, especially urine, or sometimes with visible markers, made by kicking up earth after defecating. The pack defends its territory, preventing others who are not pack members, be they dogs or humans, from entering it. And our dogs still hunt. Their predatory instinct makes anything that moves, from a mouse to a car, fair game.

Picking places
Using size as a weapon, this Samoyed tries to dominate the Pekingese. In return, the Pekingese asserts himself by biting the larger dog. Dogs learn their place in the pack through encounters such as this.

What's yours is mine...
Two French Bulldogs play a game with a toy. While dominant dogs guard their possessions, most other dogs will use them in play.

11

The Origins of the Dog

Northern giant
The Kenai wolf of Alaska, commonly weighing 135 lb (60 kg), was hunted to extinction by 1915. It probably evolved from Asian wolves, and may have been a forebear of the Alaskan Malamute dog.

Interbreeding of Asian wolf and North American timber wolf

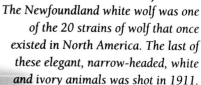

North American timber wolf

Bounty victim
The Newfoundland white wolf was one of the 20 strains of wolf that once existed in North America. The last of these elegant, narrow-headed, white and ivory animals was shot in 1911. Just under 6 ft (2 meters) long, they weighed up to 100 lbs (45 kg).

King of the forest
Timber wolves once ranged over all of North America. Native Americans tamed them and created local breeds of dogs long before the Europeans reached the continent. Today, wolves survive only in Canada and in small enclaves in the United States.

REGARDLESS OF SIZE, all dogs are directly descended from wolves. It is the range of colors, sizes, and temperaments among breeds of wolves that allowed for the dramatic variety of dogs today. That original natural variety is today sadly depleted in the wild. Wolves are intensely social animals with keen senses, who work together to catch animals larger than themselves. Their highly articulate communication and the pack behavior that they use to protect themselves are echoed today in the behavior of even the smallest of dogs.

Southern migrants
No true wolves inhabit South America. The species ventured no farther than Mexico, where a small, dark subspecies (Canis lupus baileyi) survives today. The Chihuahua and Mexican Hairless Dog are probably descended from this wolf.

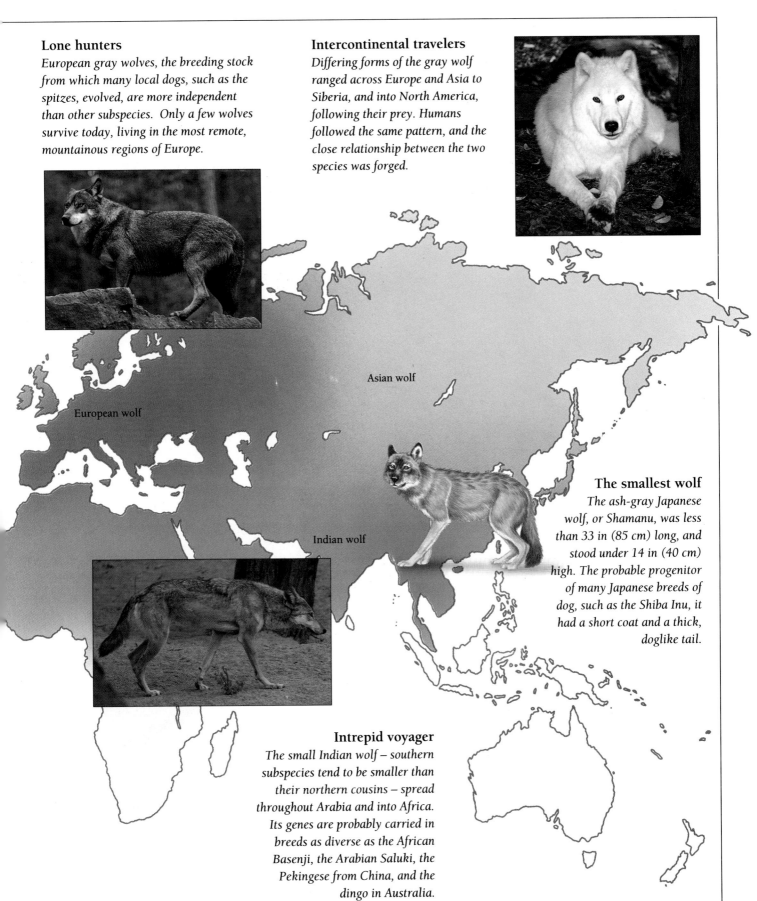

Lone hunters
European gray wolves, the breeding stock from which many local dogs, such as the spitzes, evolved, are more independent than other subspecies. Only a few wolves survive today, living in the most remote, mountainous regions of Europe.

Intercontinental travelers
Differing forms of the gray wolf ranged across Europe and Asia to Siberia, and into North America, following their prey. Humans followed the same pattern, and the close relationship between the two species was forged.

Asian wolf

European wolf

Indian wolf

The smallest wolf
The ash-gray Japanese wolf, or Shamanu, was less than 33 in (85 cm) long, and stood under 14 in (40 cm) high. The probable progenitor of many Japanese breeds of dog, such as the Shiba Inu, it had a short coat and a thick, doglike tail.

Intrepid voyager
The small Indian wolf – southern subspecies tend to be smaller than their northern cousins – spread throughout Arabia and into Africa. Its genes are probably carried in breeds as diverse as the African Basenji, the Arabian Saluki, the Pekingese from China, and the dingo in Australia.

13

From Forest to Fireside

WE FIND THE young of most species captivating, but it was the wolf cub's open willingness to become part of the human community that led our ancestors to see the value of incorporating these animals into their settlements. Wolves naturally protected their adopted human pack, alerted it to danger, and helped in the hunt. Eventually, through breeding from the tamest and most reliable stock, dogs for guarding, protecting, hunting, or simple companionship were developed. Early dogs looked much like the wolves from which they were bred, but selective breeding for specific traits has led to the variety that exists today.

Ancient companion
This Pekingese, bred over thousands of years for companionship, might seem far removed from the wolf, but it still retains bedrock wolf traits.

Built for speed
An ancient breed, this fleet-footed Pharaoh Hound is a descendant of the small wolves that once lived in the Middle East. These hounds were bred to sight and chase game.

Family features (LEFT)
Bred from the large and powerful northern timber wolf, this Samoyed retains many of the wolf's physical features. Samoyeds are good guards, growling at the sight of intruders.

Dog in sheep's clothing
(RIGHT AND FAR RIGHT)
The longhaired Briard (right) resembles the sheep it was bred to protect, the likeness acting as a camouflage to fool wolves. By the time the Belgian Sheepdog (far right) had evolved, wolves were no longer a threat, so there was no need for camouflage.

Emergency rations (LEFT)
*These Chow Chows are
descendants of guard dogs bred in
China. Their ancestors would also
have been a source of food in
times of famine.*

Dogs of war (ABOVE)
*Robust, powerful dogs like this Mastiff
were selectively bred both for defense
and for active aggression.*

Working to the gun (ABOVE)
*This German Shorthaired Pointer
happily retrieves a game bird. Even
today, we continue to use selective
breeding to create dogs with
accentuated characteristics that
fulfill our own changing needs.*

15

Coordinating Activity

PACK INSTINCT evolved to help wolves capture prey larger than themselves. To be successful in the hunt, wolves must coordinate their activities, alerting one another to scents, sights, and sounds. Cooperative behavior is still powerful in all dogs and is one reason why they make good companions. Dogs coordinate their activities not only with each other, but also with our schedules. They sleep and wake together, run and chase one another, eat collectively, and join together in greeting their leader.

Dinner party (ABOVE)
This pack of Beagles eats and drinks communally from one bowl. Because they are a true pack and know each other well, there is no competition over who eats first.

Outnumbered
Although they are far smaller than the Rhodesian Ridgeback, these dominant Chihuahuas, who know each other and form a pack of two, eat first. The larger outsider simply watches.

Mother love
These Longhaired Dachshunds look up expectantly at their owner, hoping for food or attention. They respond as they did to their mother when they were puppies. Now they coordinate their behavior to the activities of their human leader.

Working as a team
Sleeping together gives the members of a wolf pack mutual security and warmth. They all arise equally fit to work as a team. Having just awakened, these wolves become alert to a scent, sight, or sound and turn toward it. When one member of the pack finds a scent or hears a noise, his body language alerts the others. By coordinating their activities and working together, they are more alert to danger and better equipped to capture animals larger than themselves than individual wolves would be.

Unblinking stare is held

Leg is raised in anticipation

Pack members keep close together

Teamwork

WHEN GIVEN THE opportunity, dogs readily follow the pack instinct that they have inherited from wolves. The most dominant dog plays "team captain," and the rest willingly obeys its commands. The difference between a Husky team and a wolf pack is that the dogs have two team captains – the top dog and the human pack leader. True pack behavior only occurs in dogs that have lived together long enough to form relationships. Strays might travel together, but they do not coordinate their activity as closely as a sled team.

Relaxing together
The team relaxes as a group, a habit that started when, as puppies, they would huddle with their littermates for warmth. Although these dogs are not littermates, they have learned to behave in the same way with each other.

Leading from behind
The Huskies willingly follow the instructions shouted by their owner and surge ahead pulling the sled. The dogs' pack instinct inhibits disputes while they are working.

Now is no time to argue. Pull!

The tail is raised in excitement

Bodies touch as dogs strain to pull sled

Pulling together
The Huskies concentrate on working together as a team. Due to a combination of instinct and early learning, they are eager to start running as soon as they feel the harness.

Eyes are kept fixed on the trail ahead

I'm powerful, but not as powerful as you.

Paying homage to the leader (LEFT)
The top dog in the Husky pack leaps up to greet the real team leader. In all our relationships with dogs, the human must play the part of "top dog."

Taking the biscuit (ABOVE)
The pack leader leaps in the air to catch a tidbit thrown to the pack, while the rest of her team holds back. She has been chosen to be leader by her owner, but the decision was influenced by her natural authority over the other dogs.

The ears perk forward, showing anticipation

Let's get going!

Team coordinates its effort

Dogs leap forward with excitement

19

Going on Appearances

A DOG'S BEHAVIOR IS influenced by its sex and genetic background. The male puppy is masculine from birth because the development of his brain is affected by the sex hormone testosterone, which he produces while still in the womb. Under this hormonal influence he grows bigger, stronger, and more assertive than his female littermates. The female does not experience hormonal influence on behavior until her first season, usually when she is six or seven months old. Mutations in color are also related to variations in behavior in many canine species, including foxes and wolves. Selective breeding has exaggerated these, and the color of a dog's coat can partly predict its behavior.

Male has muscular body

Typical male

This male dog is more active than a female, demands more time for play, and will leave more scent markers on his territory. He is also more aggressive and destructive, and more likely to stray from home or to snap at strangers.

Typical female

This female dog demands more affection and is more companionable than the typical male dog. She is also more willing to learn obedience and easier to house train.

Overweight due to both neutering and overfeeding

Dangerous colors

Although these Cocker Spaniels are both of the same breed and sex, the golden one is more likely to develop a condition called "avalanche of rage syndrome." This causes fits of aggression, which appear with no warning and vanish just as suddenly. Cocker Spaniels of mixed colors hardly ever develop this problem.

Tail docked unnecessarily for cosmetic reasons

Nature and selection (BELOW)

Because he is male, the darker Golden Retriever is larger than the female. Selective breeding has diminished many of his dominant, aggressive male behavioral traits; neutering could reduce them still further. If the female is also neutered, she might become more dominantly aggressive.

The male has a larger head as well as a larger body

Female's body is smaller than male's

Showing Who's Boss

JUST LIKE US, dogs have a rigid social order, consisting of top dogs, challengers, dogs contented with their position, and underdogs. A wild pack of canine hunters must act as a team and kill to survive. Maintaining this "pecking order" or hierarchy is vital if fights to the death within the pack are to be avoided. The hierarchy is established through ritual displays that reveal the mental and physical strengths and weaknesses of the participants. Once dogs have learned their rank, most are content to behave within the bounds that it dictates.

Signs of appeasement (ABOVE)
Cowering and pursing her lips, this Dalmatian tells the higher-ranking German Shepherd Dog that she offers no challenge.

Show of power
A Greyhound stares intently and places his paw on a Boxer's shoulder, while she turns her head away and tries to avoid any eye contact. This ritual display reaffirms that the Greyhound is top dog and will accept no challenges.

The less dominant dog avoids eye contact

Leg rests firmly on dog's back

All right, you're in charge.

Dog turns to make escape

22

Puppy concentrates on toy

I might be small, but I'm more confident than you are.

Size is not everything (ABOVE)
Although much smaller than the Afghan Hound, this Yorkshire Terrier stands his ground and uses assertive body language to force the larger dog to back away.

Respect your elders
This Golden Retriever puppy watches while an older Labrador Retriever takes away his toy. The puppy understands that, for the time being, the mature dog has seniority of rank and can do as he likes.

Raised tail shows dominance

I bet I can outstare you.

Eye to eye
Meeting for the first time, a Pyrenean Mountain Dog and a Beagle stare at each other and sniff each other's scent. The dog that maintains eye contact the longest will exert rank seniority.

Stance shows confidence

Ancient ritual
Two wolves bare their teeth and engage in a ritualized tussle. The top wolf in a pack will meet any potential challenge to his authority by physically or psychologically asserting himself. Rank hierarchies are more complex in wolf packs than among dogs.

Playing a Part

THE PRIMARY WAY that dogs learn about their relationships with each other is through play. By playing, dogs discover one another's weak points, and learn to manipulate and hone their social skills. Play activity neutralizes the potentially dangerous situations created by dominance disputes and helps dogs to cement their pack relationships in a ritual manner. Just like us, dogs retain a lifelong enjoyment of playing and for many play is an end in itself, carried out for the fun of it.

1 Scent to investigate
First meetings are always potentially dangerous. Both of these dogs are restrained by their leashes while they scent each other. Neither dog shows aggression, but the Fox Terrier is innately superior due to his gender and greater age.

I'm the top dog around here.

2 Teasing moment (ABOVE)
The Cocker Spaniel rolls over in a manner that forestalls any possibility of aggression from the Fox Terrier. All the while, she is careful to maintain eye contact with the terrier to tell him that she is not merely being cowardly.

Leg is raised, ready to restrain the terrier

3 Playful barking
Sensing that there is no danger and still maintaining her direct eye contact, the spaniel playfully barks and bounces up toward the face of the Fox Terrier. In simple play, dogs try to mouth each other or gently chew the head region.

Let's box to see who wins.

4 Head-to-head
Both dogs are now on equal terms and, using their forelimbs, box with each other. They growl, but like most play activity, the growl is slightly "theatrical," just different enough from true growling to indicate that it is not meant in earnest.

Direct eye contact is constantly maintained

The ears flatten back to signal no serious aggressive intent

Now I know you're tougher than you look.

5 Vicious circle (LEFT)
Running in tight circles, the dogs continue their play behavior. Both try to chew at their playmate's neck. Although they met only minutes before, these two dogs have learned instantly about each other's strong and weak points.

Standing allows the dog to play from a position of strength

The Top Dog

TO ENSURE THAT the pack successfully coordinates activity, one individual must exert authority and become leader. Due to hormonal influence on behavior, the dominant dog is often male. He asserts his leadership through displays of dominance – ritualized activities that tell other dogs that a top dog is present. Although helpful, size is not the most important factor in determining who will be top dog. Dobermans and Rottweilers are naturally dominant large breeds, but many small breeds, especially terriers and dachshunds, are more dominant than breeds several times their size.

1 First sniff
A Longhaired Miniature Dachshund makes a dominant investigation of a Pekingese by sniffing her ears and mouth. His tail is raised, and his ears, which are as erect as they can become, signal the assurance of his actions.

2 Head-on-neck dominance
Placing the neck on the other dog's shoulder displays the most common form of dominant body language. Direct eye contact shows the dachshund's confidence.

3 Last things last
Having completed his investigation of the front of the Pekingese, the dachshund, still controlling the meeting, turns his attentions to the posterior region of his subject.

Lowered tail shows lack of confidence

26

1 Cocksure encounter
The body language of the authoritative dachshund includes a variety of dominant gestures. Unable to sniff the anal region of the larger dog, an Italian Spinone, he scents the prepuce (foreskin) instead. Despite his small size, the dachshund conveys his dominance by taking the lead in these investigations.

2 Problem of size
Having approached the larger spinone with great self-confidence, the dachshund has a problem actually exerting his authority. Although he is too small to dominate the spinone physically, he still actively tries to sniff his mouth.

I'll show him who's boss.

Ears are fully raised

That's better. Now I can show my higher status.

3 Exerting authority
When the spinone eventually lies down, the dominant dachshund can finally show authority. He sniffs his opponent's head region, raises the hair on his back as best he can, and dominantly stares at the eyes of the much larger, but less dominant, dog.

Meeting as Equals

ALTHOUGH ONE DOG always assumes the leadership role within a pack, this does not mean that all the other dogs in the pack will behave in a meek and passive manner. Most dogs are confident and assertive – although in a less provocative way than the top dog – and are called "subdominant" dogs. The ritual displays when they meet are subtle and often brief, allowing almost instant social activity. When two subdominant dogs first come together there is little tension, and the encounter results in either immediate play or relaxed indifference. This situation usually occurs when a puppy comes across an unfamiliar adult dog.

Loose skin protects the dog's neck

2 Rough play
The younger dog yanks a mouthful of skin and pulls. If the adult Mastiff does not repel him, the puppy learns that two dogs can meet and play without having to show overt dominance.

1 Initial encounter
This young Bloodhound trots up to a Mastiff in an unthreatening way and, forgoing ritual introductions (see pages 26–27), starts to play. Despite the fact that she knows that she is stronger, the Mastiff does not exert her dominance and allows the Bloodhound to continue his playful behavior.

Raised tail shows excitement

Tail wags to indicate no serious aggression

Behave yourself!

3 Ritual response
The Bloodhound exceeds the permitted limits, prompting the Mastiff to restrain him by gently pinning him to the ground. She does so in a ritualized manner, using physical force but little threat. The two dogs' shared subdominant status permits harmonious behavior.

Come on, let's play some more.

Relaxed ears show no threat

Hind legs are stretched into resting position

Raised tail reveals that the puppy does not feel intimidated

4 Hounded (ABOVE)
The Bloodhound understands that there has been no overtly dominant threat in the Mastiff's behavior. She has behaved "subdominantly," as he now does too by pawing at her face in an attempt to provoke a further response from her.

Will you play with me?

5 Final appeal
The meeting continues with little tension, but by now the Mastiff is showing increasing indifference to the Bloodhound's provocation. Seeing this, he rolls on his back and continues to demand that she play.

How can you resist me?

Hind legs hang limp in complete relaxation

29

The Underdog

DOGS COMMUNICATE articulately with their bodies. As a result, we find it easy to understand what dogs are saying to each other or, for that matter, to us. Submissive behavior is necessary if pack members are to follow the commands of their leader, and it is the basis for successfully incorporating dogs into our homes. Even the most dominant dogs should exhibit submissive behavior to the human members of their pack. To make more obedient companions, we have bred some dogs to always be submissive.

Relaxed submission
Many dogs, such as this Shetland Sheepdog, submit in a relaxed and contented manner when in the presence of the pack leader.

Hangdog
This Weimaraner sits down, hunches his shoulders, and droops his head and ears when he is confronted by a more dominant dog. He averts his eyes to avoid contact.

I'll obey, as long as you tell me what to do.

Crouched in submission

Tail tucked firmly between legs

Abject submission
By rolling over, with his tail tucked firmly between his legs and his lips and ears drawn back, this Yorkshire Terrier displays abject submission. Urinating while cowering is the final stage of submission.

Let's not argue.

Tactical withdrawal
By drawing back his head and lowering his whole body to the floor, a Pekingese defuses a potentially explosive situation when confronted by an equal-sized but dominant dachshund.

Ears flattened and out of danger

Appeasement gesture
Flattening back his ears, drawing back his lips, and turning his head away, this Whippet drops down on his side. He is poised to lift his foreleg in a dramatic show of submission. His tail remains close to his body, where it is out of danger.

Please leave me alone.

Forelimb raised

I'm completely defenseless and offer no threat.

Head lowered

Ears folded back

Eyes averted

31

Pack Rivalry

DOGS TREASURE POSSESSIONS and frequently want whatever another member of the pack has – simply in order to have it themselves. In these circumstances, only very dominant canines achieve their ends through aggression. For subdominant dogs, arguing over who gets the object can become a game of deftness and guile. The holder protects his prize from the other dog's jaws, but if the interloper manages to clamp his teeth on it, the two dogs enter into a tug-of-war (*see pages 76-77*). The desired object then passes back and forth between them, but the ultimate winner is often the pack member that is slightly more dominant.

1 Jealous onlooker (*ABOVE*)
While a brindle French Bulldog chews on a dog toy, his pied littermate watches enviously nearby, taking care not to make overtly dominant and provocative eye contact.

If you've got it, I want it.

Hackles (the hair on the neck) remain flat and smooth

Leaning forward, ready to lunge

Short, powerful legs give good balance

32

Ears are drawn back submissively

2 Mock play activity (ABOVE)
Because his presence has not provoked aggression, the pied French Bulldog now drops into a play position and looks directly at his sibling and at the dog chew that he desires.

Relaxed
ears signal
no anger

3 Confident grab (BELOW)
Having received no threat through either body language or voice, the pied dog confidently and quickly creeps up and grabs the toy from between the jaws of the other dog.

Toy is gripped with
the canine (eye) teeth

*Hey! That's
mine!*

4 Protecting the prize (LEFT)
Showing his mild authority, the pied dog now chews on his prize but keeps a wary eye on the brindle dog. This playful rivalry continues as the two dogs repeatedly swap the toy by athletic – and devious – moves.

Eye contact
is held

*If you want it
back, you'll
have to get it.*

33

Marking Territory

BECAUSE THE SENSE of smell is their most important sense, dogs use the odors in their waste products to stake out their territories. Some dogs kick up dirt or grass after urinating or defecating to leave a visible mark as well. Although urine is used most often to mark territory, there are odor-emitting "calling cards" in virtually all body discharges and secretions, including saliva and ear wax.

1 **Marking a scent-post**
Male dogs, such as this Tervuren (Belgian Shepherd Dog), cock their legs to urinate on upright objects, like trees. Marks are left at the nose level of other dogs. Scent lasts longer on vertical posts than it would on the ground.

Back arches to assist in effort of defecation

Odor from ears conveys social information

Lips produce a unique scent

Anal glands leave a distinctive odor on droppings

Emitting anal-gland scent
Having emptied his bowels, a Greyhound strains to squeeze his individual scent from his anal glands. Both males and females use discharge from their anal glands to leave markers; they also empty their glands when they are frightened.

The dog raises its tail, showing interest, as the scent is discovered

3 Covering tracks (ABOVE)
The setter deposits his own urine to conceal the staler smells of previous visitors. Dogs can mark up to 80 times an hour, and always have urine in reserve.

2 Reading scent messages (ABOVE)
A male Irish Setter passes the same spot and scents the urine on the tree. Liquid waste tells him whether the dog who deposited it there was male or female. If it was a female, he may be able to tell whether she was ovulating.

Making a mark
A male Golden Retriever urinates to surround himself with familiar scent. Although bitches sniff for other dogs' scents, they only mark frequently themselves when they are in season.

Tail is lifted to avoid soiling

Tree-marking in the wild
In his natural habitat, a North American timber wolf lifts a leg to mark a tree with urine, mapping out territorial boundaries so that he knows when he is back on home ground. Ritual re-marking is often carried out daily. In the unnatural indoor surroundings in which dogs find themselves, the tree is sometimes replaced by the nearest curtain.

Defending Territory

REGARDLESS OF THEIR sex or size, dogs naturally defend what they consider to be either their personal space or their pack's territory. This is why we value them as watchdogs, but the behavior can also create problems. Dogs sometimes become territorially aggressive when we do not want them to, for example when they are left in cars. There is a strong genetic component to this form of aggression, which is why it is greatest in guard breeds such as the Doberman and the German Shepherd Dog.

1 Menacing signs (LEFT AND BELOW)
A Doberman growls as he notices a Husky approaching his territory. This is the first part of ritual threat behavior. If it is not enough to inhibit the trespasser, the dog bares his teeth to display his lethal weapons.

Territorial confidence (ABOVE)
At home on his own territory, this Rottweiler-cross shows total control. With tail held confidently high and maintaining eye-to-eye contact with the intruder, he barks, shows his teeth, and advances.

Nose wrinkles as lips are drawn back to reveal teeth

2 Full threat
With his territory still under threat of invasion, the guarding dog now barks his own threats. This display still constitutes ritual aggression. Dogs usually only enter serious fights when they are necessary.

Back off or else!

Mobile territory
In his temporary territory, a German Shepherd Dog barks aggressively at what he sees to be a threat to his personal space. Dogs occasionally defend areas that they consider to be theirs, including territories as small as an armchair or other resting place. Terriers in particular often defend their owners' cars and other such territories.

Splayed ears reveal ambivalence

Ears are tilted dominantly forward

3 Dogged advance
Disregarding the Doberman's threatening behavior, the intruder advances aggressively. By not backing down in the face of ritual threats, the Husky has provoked the "home" dog to defend his territory resolutely. This confrontation is likely to break out in a fight.

You don't frighten me.

All teeth are displayed in a show of defiance

In Pursuit

WE HAVE REDUCED the dog's desire to chase and kill through selective breeding, but all dogs instinctively chase almost anything that moves because they are descended from wild hunters. This natural predatory instinct is constructively channeled in breeds such as sheepdogs and cattle dogs, allowing them to do what comes naturally, but on our behalf. They are trained to slink forward and round up livestock rather than to attack it. Without proper training, the dog's inherent inclination is to chase and bite its prey.

Tail is elevated

Look, it's running away from me!

Bicyclists' scourge (ABOVE)
The sight of a moving bicycle stimulates this dog to give chase. Because the bicyclist continues on his way, rather than stopping to challenge the dog, the canine's predatory and territorial instincts are satisfied, and chasing bicycles could easily become a habit.

Head lowered, eyes fixed on the sheep

Feet placed for sudden movement

Curled tail indicates
active excitement

Ears perk forward

If it moves...
*A jogger provokes this dog to give chase.
This can occur in any context, not just on
the dog's own territory. If the jogger
suddenly stops and challenges, the dog
learns that chasing is not always a
rewarding activity.*

*I'm going to see
him off.*

Stalking dinner
A timber wolf in winter camouflage
lowers his head and eyes his prey.
He wants to get close enough to
capture it with only a short chase.
Dogs also rarely enter into marathon
events. In the wild, the wolf pack
coordinates its predatory behavior,
but this rarely happens with dogs,
even in free-ranging packs of strays.

Chasing constructively
*A working dog (opposite)
expresses his natural instinct
and creeps up on this sheep.
The dog has been trained not
to bite. Untrained dogs often
revel in the chase and then
savage their prey.*

A Dog's Life

Dogs are sensitive to the subtlest changes around them. Using the sophisticated senses of the born predator, they observe us much more keenly than we observe them, and they pick up body-language signals that we do not even realize we are sending. For their part, they use their voices to communicate articulately in a variety of ways, howling to call other members of the pack, growling in anger, barking for joy, or whining for attention.

Dogs have all the skills of their wild ancestors. Although not as agile as cats, they are still good jumpers. They are far better swimmers – for many, there is no greater pleasure than a plunge into water. Dogs' senses are also more sophisticated than ours in many ways. They hear better than we do, an ability evolved to help them hear the rustling of a rodent on the move, which now enables them to home in on an opening fridge. Their ability to detect, locate, and identify scents is so refined that it is virtually beyond our comprehension.

Balancing acts
At the sight of food, these two terriers use different strategies to get as near to it as possible. The Scottish Terrier balances firmly on his hindquarters, and the West Highland White Terrier dances on tiptoes.

Rallying cry (ABOVE)
A German Shorthaired Pointer raises his head and emits a plaintive howl, to call to other members of his pack.

Old habits die hard
With nimble forepaws, this dog perpetuates the wolf's tactic of digging for rodents that have gone underground. Dogs dig for food, to create cool patches in which to lie, or out of boredom.

40

Curiously, just as we use perfume, dogs cover themselves in strong scent and will roll on anything with a pungent odor, including decomposing material.

Taking a sniff
Using his prodigious scenting ability, this Basset Hound sniffs the ground. Dogs can detect some scents diluted to one part per million million.

Homing in
With his head tilted so that sound reaches his ears at fractionally different intervals, this terrier perks up his ears to focus on a noise.

Being scavengers as well as predators, dogs eat a wide variety of foods, paying little attention to whether they are fresh or not. They chew sticks and bones, and some bury what they regard as excess food, to be dug up when times are hard. Because they are pack animals, they are competitive feeders. The dominant dog eats first, and all dogs wolf down their food to prevent other pack members from eating it – even if you and your family are the other pack members.

This same gregarious sociability means that dogs willingly sleep together. The sleeping positions that they assume vary with breed, age, environmental temperature, and the security that an individual feels. As well as grooming by licking, scratching, and chewing themselves, or by rolling in grass or even dust, some dogs will also groom each other.

Brushing up
A young Afghan Hound scratches her neck. Dogs groom themselves by chewing and biting at their hindquarters and scratching at their forequarters. They rub their faces with their forepaws, as cats do.

Manual dexterity
Using both forepaws, this Golden Retriever holds his chew firmly as he gnaws at it.

Vision

ALTHOUGH THEY ARE better than we are at seeing even the slightest movement at a distance, dogs' vision is not as good as ours close up. Their eyes, although not as widely placed as the wolf's, are too far apart to give accurate depth of field. Dogs have the right cells in their eyes and brain to see in color, but practically speaking, color is of little significance to them. The primary function of their eyes is to notice minimal movement and then concentrate on it intently.

The slant of the eyes lets the dog see sideways

Do I look intelligent?

Artificial intelligence
This Boxer spends each day in the reception area of my clinic. Because the placing of her eyes mimics a human face, she appears to be more intelligent than a dog with laterally placed eyes.

Dog sits still as she concentrates

I can act as eyes for my owner.

Natural eyeliner
A Husky's eyes are surrounded by dark skin. This reduces the glare of light reflected from snow, and also makes the eyes a prominent feature for communication.

Night vision
This French Bulldog can dilate his pupils more than we can, to take in more light. His eyes also contain more rods, the cells that register low light in black and white.

Pupils dilate widely to allow more light into the eye

Dog's eye view 250°–290°
Human's eye view 210°

Seeing things differently (*ABOVE*)
The dog's world differs from its owner's. We need to be able to focus on an object, see its color, and decide whether it is dangerous or safe. Frontally placed eyes with plenty of color-sensitive cone cells give us these abilities, but restrict our angle of vision. The dog's ancestors were primarily carnivorous hunters, so lateral vision was more important to them than color. Dogs' peripheral vision is more acute than ours, and their angle of vision is wider, but this varies according to how far apart their eyes are. Having fewer cone cells in their eyes than we do, their color vision is basically restricted to reds.

I'm concentrating on you.

Brown pigment on inner eyelid makes this eye look different from the other

An original gazehound
An Afghan Hound is typical of the ancient dog types originally bred for their acute vision and speed. Her eyes are more sensitive to light and movement than are ours, and their slanted positioning gives her more peripheral vision.

Raised Voices

THE AVERAGE DOG'S ability to hear is four times sharper than ours. Your dog is better at hearing high-pitched sounds, too – a requirement that evolved in its wolf ancestors, whose diet of large herbivores was supplemented with small animals, such as mice, that make high-pitched sounds. Although wolves bark an alarm signal, the dog's bark is more of a man-made characteristic, actively selected for watchdog value. Howling remains a vocal communication technique, while moaning, whimpering, and whining are perpetuated infant sounds.

We're over here. Where has everyone else gone?

Seeking attention (LEFT)
This West Highland White Terrier barks to gain attention. Barking is also used as a warning or threatening sound, in the same way that wolves bark an alarm when there is danger nearby.

Head turns to identify source of distant sound

Lips are pursed to howl

Collar tags are an efficient means of identification that should be worn by all dogs

Plaintive howl
While her partner listens intently for a reply, a Basenji howls plaintively to contact the rest of the pack. Basenjis were never selectively bred for their bark. As a result they almost never bark, limiting their sounds to a howl or the occasional yip or yelp when seriously frightened or in pain.

44

Sing-along Spinone
This Italian Spinone belongs to my nurse and spends a lot of time at my clinic, where he howls when he hears doleful songs on the radio. Many dogs howl to music just for the enjoyment of joining in. The howl is not a complaint: if they disliked the sound they would move away.

Top lip drawn down

The call of the wild
The howl is the wolf's most important vocal method of communication. Wolves howl to let other pack members know where they are. When cubs "yip" at night, adult members of the pack soon respond reassuringly with howls from wherever they are.

Did you say "Food"?

Leg is turned under in relaxed position

Ears pricked up to improve hearing

Attentive listening
Dogs sometimes tilt their heads, as this Large Munsterlander (left) and Doberman are doing, when they concentrate on listening attentively to a sound. By shifting their ear positions, they can pinpoint the location of the noise in 0.06 of a second.

A Sense of Smell

BECAUSE THE DOG'S ability to scent is extremely sophisticated, we sometimes assume that it must have some unknown "sixth sense" that helps it follow trails or find its way home. In reality, this sense is a scenting ability so acute that dogs can smell some odors diluted to one-millionth the concentration at which humans can detect them. To do this, dogs sniff air into a special chamber in the nose. This air is not washed out when the dog breathes out, so odor molecules accumulate until there are enough to smell.

You smell as if you've eaten something interesting.

Improving scent
By licking his nose, this Chow Chow increases the capture of odor molecules. There are over 200 million scent-receiving cells in a dog's nose. If spread out, the nasal membrane would cover an area greater than his body surface.

Ground scenting
A Yorkshire Terrier sniffs the ground for scent messages in another dog's urine. Like cats but unlike us, dogs have a special apparatus in the nose, the vomeronasal organ, that is responsible for the recognition of sex-related odors.

Who's the boss around here?

Ears and lipfolds are scented for information

Mutual investigation (LEFT)
Three Basenjis sniff each other as we would shake hands. Information is immediately acquired about dominance, sexual status, and position in the pack hierarchy. Because male dogs use their sense of smell to scent out females in season, they make better tracker dogs than bitches.

Air-scenting (BELOW)
Plumes of odor in the air are sniffed by an Italian Spinone. She searches for odor clues in airborne dust particles and water droplets before lifting her foreleg and "pointing" in the direction of the scent.

Anal glands produce individual scent

Body leans forward

Quiet! I can smell it over here.

Following a trail

A timber wolf follows a ground trail, possibly from prey such as deer. Dogs behave in exactly the same way. The best time for both wolves and dogs to scent is when the ground temperature is slightly higher than the air temperature, sending plumes of scent upward. This occurs in early evening, making it dogs' and wolves' preferred hunting time. The invisible scent trails are marked by the smells of damaged grass crushed underfoot and by changes in the soil, as well as by actual odors from the animal being followed.

Table Manners

UNLIKE OTHER PREDATOR species, such as cats, dogs are omnivores, eating more than just meat. They have far fewer taste buds on their tongues than we have, and are willing to consume almost anything that might offer nourishment. This willingness to try anything is combined with a sensitive vomiting reflex, which permits them to reject foods that are unpalatable or dangerous. Standard or large-size dogs are natural gorgers. Boredom, combined with too much available food, can give them weight problems. Small dogs have not evolved under the same genetic pressure, and are more likely to be selective about what they eat. Females are twice as likely to be finicky as are males.

Hands off
Protecting her food from a human as she would from other members of a canine pack, this Springer Spaniel turns and growls a warning as she is approached, natural behavior that we find socially unacceptable.

Me first, me first!

Professional beggars
Exemplifying their evolution from hunter to scavenger and beggar, these Basenjis stand on their hind legs to get near an offered morsel of food. Dogs can be trained to eat almost anything.

Don't come near me until I'm finished.

Head is held over bowl to prevent intrusion

Dog takes a firm stance to defend her food

Eyes close as dog concentrates

Mmmm. Savor the flavor.

Grass is bitten off with incisors

Careful chewing
Closing his eyes, this Shar Pei concentrates on chewing his food. Dogs will usually try anything, but they have favorites that they enjoy most.

Side salad
Grass makes a tasty snack. Some dogs are highly selective, searching out and grazing on particular grasses and weeds. Some eat vegetation only when they have an upset stomach.

Body leans forward

Tongue curls back to lap water

Lapping it up
A Boxer dips her tongue into water and forms it into a cup, throwing the liquid up into her mouth. Dogs are often very careful with precious liquids such as milk, not losing a drop, but are much sloppier with water.

Bones of Contentment

HAVING EVOLVED FROM pack animals that hunted and ate creatures larger than themselves, dogs still enjoy gnawing on large bones. Their teeth and jaw muscles are specially adapted for holding, scraping, and crushing, and they use their forepaws with great dexterity to manipulate bones and hold them in position. As a substitute for bones, most dogs willingly chew on similar objects, such as toys, edible chews, and sticks.

Getting a grip
With great dexterity, this Basenji holds a bone steady between his paws. He tilts his head, to better use his large molar teeth for gnawing on his treat.

This is tasty.

Incisors for tearing

Canines for seizing and piercing

Molars for chewing and grinding

Perfect teeth
This Bull Terrier shows the equipment vital to the carnivore. His jaw is elongated to allow plenty of space for teeth of varying sizes and uses.

Forepaws hold the chew firmly

Starting early
Although still only a few months old, this Boston Terrier chews enthusiastically on an edible stick. Chewing is instinctive behavior in all dogs.

50

Raised tail shows enjoyment

On guard
This dog drops his forequarters to the ground so that he can more readily chew his toy. He keeps his hindquarters raised, in case he has to move quickly to protect his trophy.

Be ready to move fast.

Every last bit
Gnawing on a bone, this timber wolf shows the dexterity and powerful jaw muscles that have been inherited by domestic dogs. Wolves will strip all the meat from bones, then split them open and eat the marrow. Chewing keeps their teeth, which are their most important weapons, in good condition.

A natural toothbrush
This Golden Retriever holds his object with crossed paws and gnaws at it. Chewing hard objects cleans his teeth, and is necessary to maintain healthy teeth and gums.

I've done this for years.

One paw holds the chew firmly on the other

Buried Treasure

THE DOG'S INSTINCT to cache food, creating a reserve for time of need, is inherited from wolves. It leads well-fed, totally domesticated dogs to bury bones and then dig them up later. In the absence of bones, dogs may bury food such as bone-shaped biscuits, and some will try digging in the carpet if there is no earth available. Dogs are efficient earth movers and will also dig to flush out small animals that have gone underground; to escape confinement; and to create a cool patch of earth in which to lie.

I can smell something.

Dog starts digging with one paw

There's something down here.

Expression shows intense concentration

1 Scent marks the spot
Although it is over a month since she buried her bone here, this dog finds the site through scent. The smell of the bone percolates through the ground.

2 Getting warmer
The smell of the bone intensifies as the dog digs, and she becomes more intent. Some breeds, such as terriers, were bred to dig out small animals in this way.

Marrow is licked from the bone

3 One at a time
The hole is now too deep for digging with both forepaws simultaneously. The dog changes technique and dips in with one paw to drag out earth with a scooping action. Completely ambidextrous, most dogs will use both forepaws in turn. Similarly, forepaws and hindpaws will be used equally when filling the hole.

What's that I feel?

4 Success!
Having found her prize, she reaches in and pulls it out in her mouth. Burying and then digging up food provides natural mental and physical activity for dogs. Denying them these outlets can lead to unwanted destructive behavior.

Raised tail reveals heightened excitement

Leg is drawn out for balance and to tip the head down to reach the bone

6 Enjoying the meal
Having recovered her treasure, the dog settles down for a good gnaw. Dogs willingly chew on the filthiest of finds, but in this instance the dog's fastidious owner has cleaned the bone. The hole in the ground remains. It will only be filled in if she chooses to bury the bone again after having her chew.

5 Any more?
Even after finding her cache, this dog's digging instinct has been so aroused that she continues to paw at the hole. The scent rising from the earth is now at its most powerful, and she might be checking for more buried food.

Rolling

MANY MAMMALS ROLL on their backs either to groom themselves or for what appears to be simple pleasure. Dogs indulge in this behavior when they are contented and feel they are in no danger. Your dog is most likely to roll after it has become wet in the rain or after a swim. Some dogs are especially fond of carrying out this activity in sand or dry earth. Rolling for fun or to groom is a distinct activity from rolling in foul-smelling scent. We can only guess why dogs choose to muck-roll, but it is likely that, like wolves, they do so to mask their own scent.

Pleasure roll (BELOW)
With joyful abandon, a Chow Chow rolls onto his back, pedaling his legs in the air. At the same time, he arches his back up and down, and flips his head from side to side. It seems he does so for the pure pleasure of it.

Life is a joy!

1 **Catching the scent** (ABOVE)
Coming across another animal's droppings, an Italian Spinone stops to capture the scent in his nose. This will be your first sign of premeditated rolling.

Fox droppings are sniffed

Legs kick up in apparent delight

54

Rolling on scent
In exactly the same way as your dog rolls in what we consider to be offensive-smelling muck, a timber wolf in the wild may roll its forequarters in decomposing material that is producing strong odors, such as a rotting carcass. Many natural hunters cover themselves in foreign odors, most probably to hide their own scent from their quarry. Their prey have sensitive noses, and are less alarmed by odors such as animal droppings or decomposing material than they are by the wolf's own body scents, which they will recognize as those of a predator.

Mmm...smells like a good disguise.

2 Anointing one shoulder (LEFT)
Rather than joyfully flinging himself on the ground, the spinone carefully places one shoulder on the offensive substance and rubs it. Some dogs carry out a full roll, then stand up and sniff the substance again before performing a second roll.

Head is turned and side of face is rubbed in scent

3 Balancing the smell (RIGHT)
Having covered one shoulder in pungent scent, the dog now methodically places his other shoulder on the animal droppings to make sure that the odor is symmetrically placed on both sides of the body. After completing this stereotypical behavior, he might indulge in a pleasurable roll.

Neck and ear are rubbed in scent

Half-standing, the dog can anoint his shoulders accurately

Keeping Clean

OGS LICK, SCRATCH, chew, and shake themselves to keep tidy. Occasionally, they groom each other as well. Shaking is the most simple and frequent grooming procedure for your dog. After resting, being handled, and, most commonly, getting wet, dogs will often vigorously shake their hair back into its natural position. They also lick their coats and pull out any objects that become entangled in the fur. Some dogs trim their nails by chewing them and use their dewclaws (the remnant of a dog's "thumb," found on the inner side of each foot) to clean their ears. Body openings are meticulously licked clean, especially if there are discharges from them.

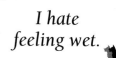

I hate feeling wet.

Tumble dry
After a bath, a Bouvier des Flandres puppy vigorously shakes the water from his coat. If he did not do this, the water would eventually penetrate through his almost waterproof undercoat.

Water is flung out from fur

Ears show alertness

Ear wax is licked

I wonder what you taste like?

Mutual grooming
A male Japanese Akita licks the ear and other head regions of a young Cocker Spaniel bitch. Licking is usually part of maternal behavior. This type of grooming has distinct sexual associations.

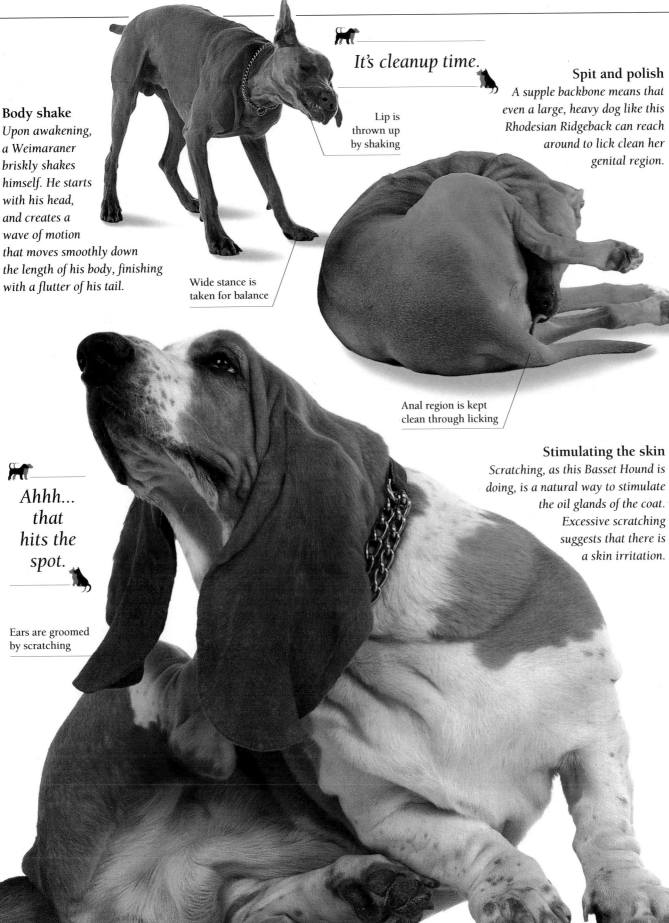

It's cleanup time.

Body shake
Upon awakening, a Weimaraner briskly shakes himself. He starts with his head, and creates a wave of motion that moves smoothly down the length of his body, finishing with a flutter of his tail.

Lip is thrown up by shaking

Wide stance is taken for balance

Spit and polish
A supple backbone means that even a large, heavy dog like this Rhodesian Ridgeback can reach around to lick clean her genital region.

Anal region is kept clean through licking

Stimulating the skin
Scratching, as this Basset Hound is doing, is a natural way to stimulate the oil glands of the coat. Excessive scratching suggests that there is a skin irritation.

Ahhh... that hits the spot.

Ears are groomed by scratching

57

Sleeping and Snoozing

BECAUSE DOGS NATURALLY coordinate their activities to human timetables, your dog is likely to sleep when you do. With a greater need for sleep than we have, dogs also take "cat-naps," spending half of each day relaxed with their eyes closed. These extra rest periods occur when the pack leader relaxes. Most sleeping time is light sleep, from which the dog awakens easily, but 20 percent is deep sleep, which is when dogs dream.

Hot dog
By stretching out his hind legs behind him, a Maltese Terrier exposes as much as possible of his body surface to the cool floor. This is a puppy trait that is sometimes retained into adulthood.

Long hair can make it hard to see expression

I'm bushed!

Ears are relaxed

Tongue curls as dog yawns

Creature comfort
A natural comfort-seeker, this Rhodesian Ridgeback has curled up to keep warm in the most comfortable place she can find. Yawning occurs *when dogs are completely relaxed, especially just before closing their eyes to sleep, but it can also be a sign of nervousness and apprehension.*

This is so comfortable.

Let sleeping dogs lie (RIGHT)
Like this Yorkshire Terrier, which is dozing next to a human companion, most dogs like to sleep against an object that protects their backs. Dominant dogs, however, avoid contact when sleeping and prefer to lie alone.

Hind paws are turned out

Forelegs become limp

Legs hang relaxed

Complete relaxation
After vigorous activity, this Golden Retriever puppy rolls over on his back before falling asleep. This leaves his vulnerable belly unprotected. Only dogs that feel totally secure will sleep in this way.

What? Me worry?

Lone wolf
Showing no fear, the leader of a wolf pack stretches out in the sun and sleeps alone. Usually, he first turns around in circles to flatten the area that he will lie on. When he falls into deep, dreaming sleep, his legs might paddle, his whiskers flicker, and his eyelids flutter. Even while asleep, his jaws can move and his voice can be activated, just as can happen when your dog is in a deep sleep.

On the Move

OGS ARE BUILT for stamina, so they can work over protracted periods of time. When left to travel on their own, they often trot or canter rather than simply walk. Galloping, however, is reserved for the short bursts of speed needed when chasing, playing, or burning off excess energy. Almost all breeds have supple spines that make them good at tight spaces, but only well-muscled, long-legged breeds like Greyhounds show grace when racing. Others can be quite clumsy.

Flat out
Because he is a true dwarf – with a normal-size body but short legs – this Basset Hound appears clumsy as he gallops. Even so, he can still outrun all but the very fastest humans.

Maximum power and I'm airborne.

Brakes on!

Quick change
An Afghan Hound abruptly changes direction as he runs. This nimbleness of foot evolved to follow the zigzag movements of natural prey such as rabbits.

Forelegs hang relaxed

Feet land close together

Power lifting
With the grace of a ballet dancer, this Wirehaired Fox Terrier uses the powerful muscles of his hind legs to leap from the ground. Some dogs can leap to three times their own height (see pages 62–63).

Balancing act
A timber wolf shows the natural balance inherited by all dogs. He can stand on his hind legs for some time, either to scent the air or to get nearer to what interests him. Where footing is solid, wolves and dogs are adequate climbers, but they usually restrict themselves to clambering over obstacles rather than aspiring to true climbing.

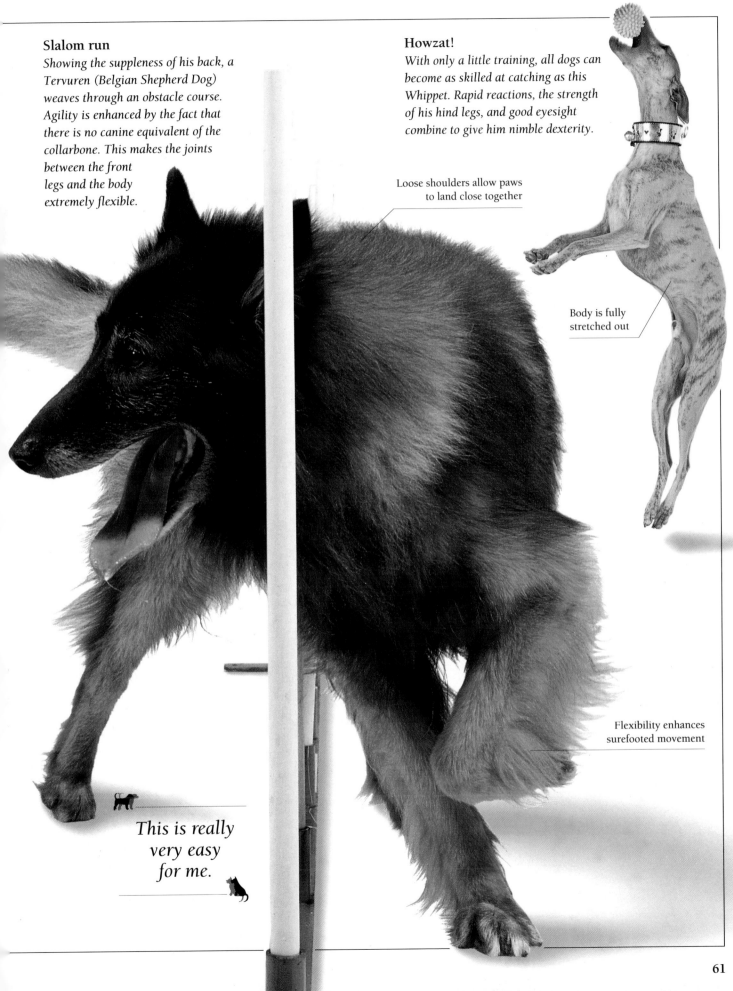

Slalom run

Showing the suppleness of his back, a Tervuren (Belgian Shepherd Dog) weaves through an obstacle course. Agility is enhanced by the fact that there is no canine equivalent of the collarbone. This makes the joints between the front legs and the body extremely flexible.

Howzat!

With only a little training, all dogs can become as skilled at catching as this Whippet. Rapid reactions, the strength of his hind legs, and good eyesight combine to give him nimble dexterity.

Loose shoulders allow paws to land close together

Body is fully stretched out

Flexibility enhances surefooted movement

This is really very easy for me.

Jumping

Most dogs are surprisingly good jumpers. All but the heaviest breeds and those with short legs are able to jump several times their own height. Dogs will jump spontaneously when they are suddenly confronted by an obstruction such as a ditch or fence. If they have more time, they eye the obstacle and measure their stride before jumping over it. Almost all dogs want to jump, but it can be dangerous for some of them. Giant breeds can suffer internal injuries if they land too heavily, and overweight dogs can tear the ligaments in their hind legs.

2 Airborne
Now in the air, the dog starts to draw up his hind legs. At all times he keeps his eyes focused on the object of his attention. Concentrating too hard on jumping might make him miss his objective.

Legs are tucked tightly into body

1 Cleared for take-off
Using his powerful hind-leg muscles, this Rottweiler-cross propels himself off the ground. At the same time, he draws in his front legs to avoid injuring them, creating an ideal aerodynamic shape.

Paws extended ready for contact

Paws leave ground when body is fully stretched

That's a good, gentle landing.

Eye contact is maintained

Tail curls
forward for
balance

*I'm keeping my
eyes on what
I want.*

3 Over the top
*Having reached his
projected altitude, the dog
continues to draw in his
hind legs but now starts
to extend his forelimbs.*

4 Starting descent
*The dog now uses his tail
more, curling it forward to
assist his balance. He continues
to focus his attention on his
target as he comes down.*

Legs are held almost
straight in descent

Shoulders absorb
impact of landing

5 Coming in to land
*The dog's front legs reach down
with flat paws, for landing. The hind
legs are still fully extended, having
been raised high to prevent injuries.*

Forelimbs
land firmly

6 Down to earth
*With his forefeet firmly planted
on the ground, the dog draws his
hind legs forward as far as possible.
This provides him with maximum
propulsion as he continues to run.*

Paws reach out
for landing

AT HOME WITH US

Schooltime
Concentrating on the reward that will follow, this Golden Retriever sits on command. Both dogs and owners benefit from simple games such as this.

DOGS SETTLE INTO our lives easily because their body rhythms are similar to ours. They sleep when we do, are active when we are, and learn both their own and our feeding times to the minute. There can, however, be problems. Some dogs try to dominate their human companions. Without natural outlets for their sex drives, many male dogs eye legs or sofa cushions as fair game. Neutering can remedy some habits without dramatically changing a dog's personality, but it cannot cure all unwanted behavior.

Close for comfort
Dogs are inveterate comfort-seekers and social animals, enjoying themselves most when the "pack" is together.

As pack leader, it is your attention that your dogs seek. They rely on you for mental and physical stimulation. You feed them, groom them, house them, play with them, and protect them. In turn, all of their behavior involves you.

Learning manners
On meeting a cat, this Border Collie's urge is to chase, but dogs must inhibit some instincts to share our homes.

Flexible friends
Bred as outdoor working dogs, these Huskies move into a home setting as readily as any other dogs. This elasticity of behavior is the reason why dogs have so successfully integrated themselves into our lives.

Because we are "top dogs," we can teach our pets – they learn to herd flocks, or to turn aggression on and off on command – but we actively teach dogs only part of what they know. Throughout life, dogs observe the world and teach themselves, and then act on what they learn. Some dogs become jealous if their leader shows affection to another dog or even another human. Others become possessive over their food or toys, and threaten not only other dogs, but also members of their human family if they come near. As they age, many dogs become more dependent upon their owners. Routine becomes an end in itself, and any change worries them.

Dogs' facial expressions are similar to ours, which helps us to understand when they are happy or sad, bored or alert – although we can misinterpret their actions. Dogs can be destructive when agitated, excited, or worried. We sometimes think this behavior is willful, but in fact it is usually an expression of anxiety. To make the most of our dogs, we and they must understand where they fit into our home lives.

Ultimate joy
Rolling over and baring her belly, this Brittany Spaniel shows subservience. She is rewarded by the pleasure of having her chest rubbed.

A Dog's Home

WITH THEIR dramatic ability to adapt to a wide variety of circumstances, most dogs have no difficulty in coping with a primarily indoor existence. As sociable creatures, they crave our company and integrate themselves into our routines. The home is their territory, and the human members of the household their pack. Dogs retain virtually all their natural behavior indoors: they exercise themselves, investigate objects, and function as part of a pack. Inveterate pleasure-seekers, dogs seek out the most comfortable lifestyle possible and sometimes vigorously defend it.

I trust you; you protect me.

Greetings
Seeing his pack leader sitting down, this Cocker Spaniel goes over, stands on his hind legs, and acknowledges his owner's superiority by trying to reach up to him.

Freedom of movement (LEFT)
As household pets, most dogs are denied the freedom of going in and out when they please, and live in what amount to luxurious prisons. Using a cat-flap as his personal entrance and exit, this Yorkshire Terrier can decide when he wants to be indoors or out.

Sitting brings the owner's face closer to the dog

Relaxed facial expression

Stands comfortably on hind legs

66

Ears are laid in relaxed position

It just feels right carrying things.

Daily routine (LEFT)
Bred to retrieve, a Golden Retriever fulfills his "fetching" instinct in the home by collecting the mail each morning. Less conveniently, some dogs do the same with our personal items.

Tail raised for balance

Indoor exercise (RIGHT)
A lack of natural outlets for expending energy causes this Cocker Spaniel to burn up his energy indoors. Your dog may become destructive if it is not given enough exercise.

If you come any nearer, I'll get fierce.

Family quarrel
When challenged to move off a bed that he considers to be his own personal space, this small terrier bares his teeth and threatens his owner.

Dominant stare is held

Scavenging

YOUR DOG IS likely to take food wherever – and whenever – it finds it. Scavenging is rewarding, because it meets the dog's need to hunt and seek its own food as well as satisfying its thirst and hunger. Because they have fewer taste buds than many other animals, dogs will eat whatever is at hand. If they are hungry, they will take decomposing meat and even animal droppings. "Stealing" food is perfectly natural behavior, which is why it can be difficult to train dogs not to scavenge at home. Dogs certainly do not believe they are stealing the food.

Let's see if there's anything tasty to eat in here.

Drink problem (LEFT)
After checking that no one is about, a Weimaraner takes the opportunity to lap up tea from a mug left on the floor. Most dogs will risk trying the taste of almost anything.

Head disappears as dog investigates the bag thoroughly

Searching the shopping
Finding an unattended shopping bag satisfies this Cocker Spaniel's need to hunt and eat. Many dogs consume whatever they can find, which explains why about 30 percent of dogs are overweight.

Docked tail wags with excitement

68

Cleaning up

Having come across a rotting carcass, two timber wolves scavenge what meat they can from it. Although wolves primarily hunt for their food, they will also scavenge when hungry. Through centuries of selective breeding, we have successfully reduced the dog's desire to hunt while accentuating its willingness to scavenge. Today, in some parts of the world, scavenging is one of the common reasons why dogs are tolerated. Their robust stomachs and strong desire for food make them perfect natural waste-disposal units.

Guess who's coming to dinner!

Long coat can conceal body language

Uninvited guest
Not having been trained that it is anti-social behavior in human terms, a Briard naturally – and innocently – stands up to eat a meal straight off the dinner plate that she has spotted.

69

First Encounters

CANINES ENJOY COMPANY. By introducing ourselves into their lives almost at birth, we convince dogs that humans make friendly companions. The same technique can be used to integrate any other species into a dog's life. It is best to do this when the dog is less than 12 weeks old. After that age, greater care must be taken to ensure that neither its natural predatory instincts nor its fear of strange animals is stimulated.

Herd reaction
Breeds used in agriculture, such as these Australian Shepherds, will naturally try to herd livestock like these goats. Herding is simply the dog's chasing instinct modified through human intervention.

Eye contact is held

Ears are perked forward, showing active interest

You're just like my littermates.

Early encounter
A young puppy examines a kitten, which confidently holds its ground. By meeting cats now, this puppy becomes less likely to chase them when he is older.

Leg is raised as puppy starts to withdraw from kitten

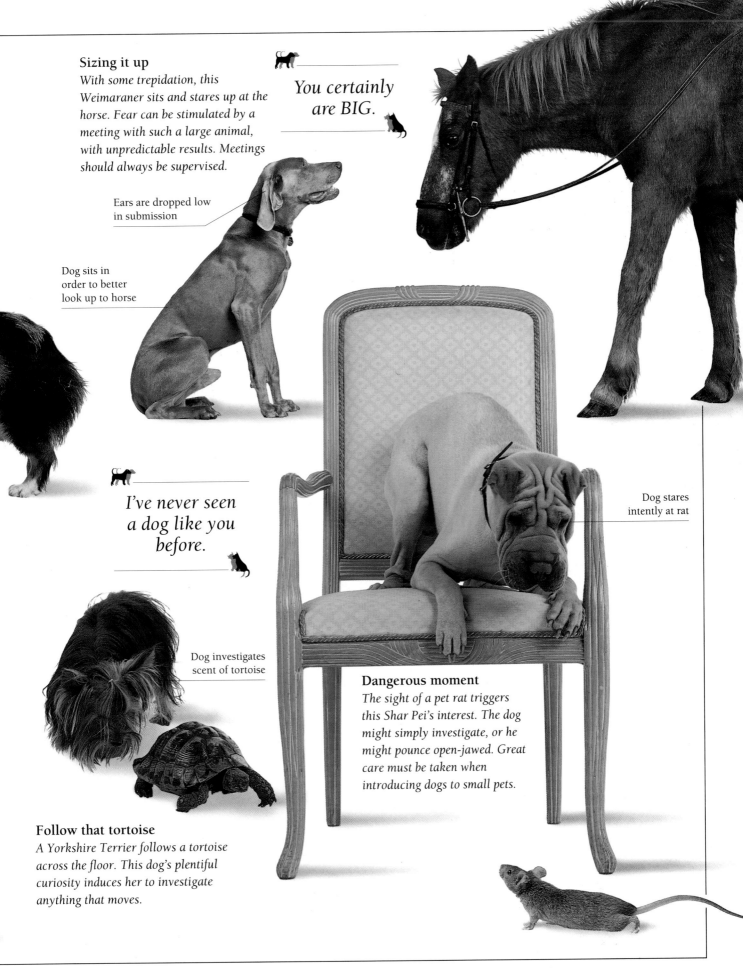

Sizing it up
With some trepidation, this Weimaraner sits and stares up at the horse. Fear can be stimulated by a meeting with such a large animal, with unpredictable results. Meetings should always be supervised.

You certainly are BIG.

Ears are dropped low in submission

Dog sits in order to better look up to horse

Dog stares intently at rat

I've never seen a dog like you before.

Dog investigates scent of tortoise

Dangerous moment
The sight of a pet rat triggers this Shar Pei's interest. The dog might simply investigate, or he might pounce open-jawed. Great care must be taken when introducing dogs to small pets.

Follow that tortoise
A Yorkshire Terrier follows a tortoise across the floor. This dog's plentiful curiosity induces her to investigate anything that moves.

71

Seeking Attention

BECAUSE THEY ARE so gregariously sociable, and because they consider us to be their pack leaders, dogs crave our attention. Being touched is soothing and reassuring for dogs, just as it is for us. Stroking your dog reduces its blood pressure, its heart rate, and its skin temperature. It calms its sense of arousal. Dependent dogs demand attention most, but even dominant, aggressive canines solicit attention from a strong human leader.

Pick me up, I'm worried.

Leg raised as high as possible

Soft touch
A Weimaraner raises a forepaw to tap his owner and get attention. Dogs can be trained to "shake hands" from this basic gesture.

Hey, look, I'm here.

Emotional blackmail
This Chihuahua stands and scratches at his owner's leg to get his attention. Although this is a sign of submission, dogs such as this in fact often dominate their owners into picking them up.

Head is raised to bark or howl

Double demands
While her owner reads, one of these Golden Retrievers woofs to attract attention. The other gathers herself as close as possible, hoping to be comforted through touch.

Cheek-to-cheek
Seeking his owner's attention, this Gordon Setter puts his face as close as he can to hers. Although elderly, he is mimicking the way he behaved as a puppy with his mother.

Dog enjoys body contact

I do hope she strokes me.

Dog presses herself against chair

Jealously Guarded

ALL DOGS NATURALLY guard and protect what they consider to be theirs. They often behave possessively about prized objects, sleeping locations, or even the attentions of special people. Children are not seen as dominant, and may therefore be confronted with this dangerous form of aggression. Because of this, adults must always supervise meetings between dogs and children.

Purse-mouthed command bark

1 The voice of annoyance
Seeing the other dog playing with a toy, this Golden Retriever barks to demand the toy for herself.

Head is thrust forward assertively

I want it because you have it.

2 Visual threat (ABOVE)
The retriever continues to threaten and bares her teeth. Responding to this display, the Italian Spinone drops the toy and looks at the aggressor.

3 Winning possession
Showing submission to the more powerful retriever, the spinone rolls over, leaving the toy unattended. The retriever can now take possession of the toy.

Submissive roll

74

Guarding his prize
Standing over his meal, this dominant timber wolf threatens anyone or anything that comes near. He will continue to do so until his hunger is satisfied. Similar behavior occurs in dogs, and is not dependent on sex or breed. Terriers are known for being possessive, but even a gentle breed such as the Golden Retriever guards food. Often, a dog is possessive of the attention of its owner, behaving aggressively toward any potential rival.

Guarding food
To prevent the loss of any of his food, this German Shepherd Dog puppy threatens the tan puppy, who submissively backs away. The German Shepherd Dog puppy is dominant because of his size and his temperament.

Don't you dare come near. It's mine.

Body pulls away

Eyes look away to show submission

Puppy moves forward confidently

Tests of Strength

TUG-OF-WAR IS A DOG'S favorite sport. It serves a variety of purposes. Some dogs are jealous of others' possessions and want to have them. Others play tug-of-war for the simple fun of the game, with no end purpose other than pure enjoyment. In normal circumstances the self-confident dog ultimately wins, but sometimes superior dogs playing with others lower in the hierarchy let the underdog win, simply to prolong the activity. Tug-of-war reinforces social positions among dogs that live together, so if people enter into the game, they should always make sure that they show high rank by winning.

Winner takes all
This retriever puppy watches the dachshund marching away with the toy. A game has ended with the dachshund taking permanent possession of the prize.

Dog looks back to ensure that the puppy does not follow

Canine teeth are used to grip toy

... and you're not getting it back.

Toy is gripped firmly

Equal and opposite (*ABOVE*)
This Golden Retriever and Italian Spinone stand side-by-side as they try to get a better grasp on their toy. These dogs are equal in size and confidence. Tugging is simply a game, and is not being used to exert authority.

I love contact sports.

Youth and age
While this older Labrador Retriever tries to pull the toy away, the young Golden Retriever runs in and grabs it. Although adult dogs are usually gentle with puppies, situations like this can lead to displays of possessive aggression.

Head is lowered
defensively

Final whistle
*A growl from the dominant dog tells the
other one that the game is over. In
canine terms, possession is now final.*

Just for fun
*Showing complete relaxation and
indicating that this game of tug-of-
war is for sheer pleasure, one dog lies
flaccidly on his back while the other
tugs on their toy.*

*Bet you can't get it
away from me.*

Something to prove
*Bracing his hind legs, this puppy gives the toy a
fierce pull. If he wins this game of tug-of-war with
a human, his self-confidence increases.*

Toy is
playfully
pulled away

Leg lifts as dog
jumps away

Legs braced
ready to pull back

Stirring things up
*To provoke a response from her partner, this
Basenji teasingly shakes the toy. The other
dog responds by grabbing at it. Specially
made dog toys are best for these games.*

77

Games with People

ALTHOUGH DOGS ARE often content just to enjoy the luxuries of life with us, they still need mental and physical activity. It is in their nature to be constantly alert, and under natural circumstances they are keen observers of the world around them. Without activity they become bored, and bored dogs can be destructive. Playing games with canines keeps their minds active and – if you play the right types of games – stimulates their bonding to you and reaffirms your role as pack leader.

Playing to win
A terrier pulls possessively on a toy made specially for tugs-of-war. Dogs, especially dominant ones, should never be allowed to win at this game when playing with humans. If they do, it enhances their feeling of dominance.

Harmonious relationship (BELOW)
Hearing his owner sing, a Basset Griffon Vendeen joins in the chorus. Seemingly frivolous activities such as this actually serve to strengthen the bond between you and your dog.

Lips are pursed to howl

A difficult catch (ABOVE)
This Wirehaired Fox Terrier must concentrate to play successfully with such a large ball. Because the ball is too big for him to catch in his mouth, he learns to move it with his muzzle. Teaching this game is the prelude to "playing football" with your dog.

Balloon bounces off dog's nose

Paw is raised to touch tentatively

It jumps away every time I touch it!

Hide-and-seek
This mature Gordon Setter enjoys pawing his owner when she "hides" from him. Playing hide-and-seek with people or toys stimulates the dog's natural desire to search and investigate.

Ears show alertness

Eye contact is maintained

Forelegs are used to balance

It may not be a bird, but it's still fun to chase.

Legs prepared to land softly

Dog starts to follow the balloon

Mission almost impossible
By jumping at a virtually uncatchable balloon, these dogs are given the opportunity to use their ingenuity while at the same time exercising their bodies. They depend on you to provide the object of the game and to act as referee.

Happy Dogs

WE CAN TELL when dogs are happy by watching their mobile ears, bright eyes, wagging tails, and expressive body language. This is hardly surprising, because they share many expressions and emotions with us. Dogs cannot, however, smile. When they pull back their lips in a greeting they are acting in a subservient manner as they would to a canine pack leader, although occasionally some dogs do learn to mimic a human smile. Dogs need not be excited to be happy: contentment and relaxation also bring pleasure.

Wrinkling the nose makes the dog sneeze

Legs are held in begging position

Hind paws are splayed out for balance

The height of delight
Standing tall, this Miniature Poodle shows her pleasure by walking on her hind legs. This brings her closer to the object of her attention, the face of her owner.

Accomplished mimic
Although he looks fierce, this Dandie Dinmont Terrier is simply copying a human smile. This is learned behavior, not inherited.

Mother love
A young wolf rests his head on his mother's back. Happiness is a human definition, but there is little doubt that this wolf is relaxed and contented. Dogs are also happy in this way when life is pleasurable and enjoyable, and sad when denied physical activity, mental stimulation, or contact with their human "family" or other dogs. There is a direct link between emotions and health: sadness or depression can lead to poor health in humans, and the same probably applies to dogs. It is healthy to be happy.

Open offer (BELOW)
Wagging his tail and lifting his leg, a Golden Retriever subserviently exposes his belly and asks to be stroked. Dogs that are happy in a stable relationship with their owners are likely to show this kind of relaxed behavior.

Relaxed contentment (RIGHT)
This pleasure-seeking Golden Retriever has ensconced himself in the most comfortable place he can find. Dogs need mental stimulation, but are also happy when they are relaxed and at ease.

Legs are relaxed

Tail hangs limp

Belly is exposed

Sheer bliss.

Joy ride (BELOW)
These Bearded Collies find it exciting to stick their heads out of the car window. Although this is a potentially dangerous habit, most dogs enjoy it because the sensation of wind on their faces mimics the enjoyment of a high-speed chase.

Heads and Tails

THE "NATURAL" DOG has a long tail, a moderately long muzzle, and erect ears. Dogs use these to signal their feelings, but we sometimes make the signals more difficult to understand by altering dogs through breeding or surgery. Modifications were first made to enhance dogs' work abilities: for example, spaniels' tails were docked to prevent entanglement when retrieving game. Today, there is no justification for such alterations – they are carried out solely for fashion.

A docked tail moves more rapidly than a natural one

Tail curls as it wags

Complete apparatus
This Doberman madly wags his intact tail to show happiness or excitement. Many Dobermans still have their ears and tails cut. There is no medical reason for this: it is carried out solely to make the dog appear more ferocious.

Tail tucked firmly between the legs

Submissive pose
By tucking his tail between his legs, this Whippet simply, but dramatically, signals submissiveness. This obvious gesture is unlikely to be misunderstood.

82

Human features (LEFT)
This Boxer exemplifies the flattened, "human" face of many breeds. Her ears are intact, although cropping is still carried out on this breed in some countries, but her tail has been docked.

You can see what I'm feeling, can't you?

Ready to go (BELOW)
Keeping direct eye contact with his owner, this Greyhound lays back his ears and pants. These are signals of submissive anticipation to his human pack leader.

Lips are pulled back submissively

Ears show alertness

Panting with excitement

Blind enthusiasm
With his ears perked forward and his natural tail erect and wagging, this Australian Silky Terrier is obviously alert. Long hair over his eyes sometimes interferes with visual communication.

Firm, erect stance shows confidence

A wagging tail indicates excitement

Panting rids the body of excess heat

Getting Worked Up

CANINE EXTROVERTS BEHAVE in a relentlessly gregarious way, but so do highly strung or neurotic individuals. Prolonged boredom can also induce overexcitement. The tendency to be excitable is partly inherited and partly learned. It is one of the prime characteristics for which dogs have been selectively bred. Terriers exemplify the most excitable breeds, and hounds like Bassets and Bloodhounds the least excitable. Excitement is a gratifying feeling. It acts as its own reward, which is one reason why dogs learn to behave this way.

The doorbell! Something exciting is going to happen!

Tail wags with excitement

Overeager greeting

This excitable Springer Spaniel responds to the sound of the doorbell by instantly leaping up at the door as if shot from a cannon. Her actions are rewarded when the visitor enters, and this reinforces her behavior.

Ardent excitement

Excited by the presence of another dog, this Tibetan Terrier clasps the Miniature Schnauzer and indulges in mock sex activity. Although males behave this way to show dominance, both males and females will mount other dogs when overexcited.

Don't you dare leave.

The long goodbye
Seeing his owner about to depart, this Cocker Spaniel growls and snaps at his trousers. The dog feels he can dictate what his owner does, and becomes recklessly excitable when he anticipates an unwanted departure.

Powerful greeting
A Leonberger jumps up to greet his owner, just as he jumped to greet his mother as a puppy. Many dogs become overexcited when they see their "leaders," which can be dangerous behavior from a dog as massive as this.

Body stretches to reach face

Nubile knee
Overexcited by seeing his owner, this Golden Retriever grabs his leg and uses it as a sex object. Dogs often behave this way when excited by the arrival of strangers in their homes.

Not very sexy-looking, but it's all I've got.

85

Bored Dogs

DOGS DO NOT like being alone. They are a sociable species, and it is unnatural for them not to have companionship or activity. A dog needs to be mentally active for about half of its time, and if it is not its brain actually shrinks in size. Most bored dogs just look glum and lie around, but many become destructive. They dig under fences, burrow in the carpet, and scratch at walls. A playmate is the surest solution, but even this does not always work. Because we keep dogs in artificial surroundings, their mental well-being is as much our responsibility as their physical health.

Abject boredom (LEFT AND RIGHT)
With nothing better to do, this Hungarian Viszla climbs onto a chair, yawns, looks glum, and shuts her eyes. Her brain and temper will benefit from mental stimulation.

Not in the mood
An Italian Spinone refuses a Boston Terrier's request to play. Another dog is usually a reliable cure for boredom, but not the only way. We should anticipate our pet's needs and create mentally and physically demanding activities for them.

Flaccid, hanging ears show lack of interest

Sorry, but I'm not interested.

Classic play-bow

86

Something to do
With nothing to stimulate his mind, a Cocker Spaniel gnaws on a chew while his partner looks on. Rubbing your hands on your dog's toys increases the likelihood that the toys will be chewed, rather than your furniture.

Unoccupied dog watches the toy

Can I have a try at that?

Legs are extended back in relaxed position

Mental torpor
This glum-looking Golden Retriever is content to simply watch the world go by. He rests because he is cut off from the moment-to-moment stimulation he would find outdoors.

Life's a drag.

Tail hangs limp

Craving Company

IF A DOG IS left on its own, without physical or mental stimulation, a dog can develop stereotypical routines. Just like a caged wolf in a zoo, it might pace relentlessly, or it might run up and down the stairs, bark incessantly, or even urinate and defecate in the house. Separation anxiety and this kind of obsessive behavior occur most frequently in dogs rescued from animal shelters.

Carpet is shaken as if it is prey

Destructive worrying
This German Shepherd Dog vents his frustration on a carpet. Dogs can behave totally out of character when left alone, chewing and tearing things, and digging and soiling anywhere in the house. These are signs of anxiety, not actions of retribution for being left alone.

Signs of change
This Great Dane sees the suitcase and immediately starts worrying. Dogs are creatures of routine; they observe us closely and note any changes in our activities. The Great Dane does not necessarily understand that a suitcase means her owner is going away – although dogs can quickly learn this association – but she does know that her routine has changed, and begins to worry.

88

Where is everybody?

Solitary confinement
In the absence of more constructive activities, this Golden Retriever shreds the newspaper that has just been delivered. If he is still unhappy over being left at home alone he might start licking his forepaws obsessively, to the extent that he will need medical attention.

Well, there's nothing else to do.

Dog relaxes as it chews

Distress call (ABOVE)
Certain breeds, such as this Doberman, are more prone to separation anxiety than others and howl plaintively when they feel they have been "deserted." Barking, especially continuous, rhythmic barking, is one of the most common manifestations of the frustration dogs feel at being left alone.

Fight or Flight

WHEN CONFRONTED with the unknown, dogs show their fear in one of three ways. Their first reaction is usually to try to flee or at least hide. If this is not possible, dogs have two options: to fight or to collapse in a submissive heap. Even the most dominant dog can be frightened by strange sights or sounds, larger animals, or anything new and unexpected. Fear can be learned, but it is also an inherited trait in some breeds, such as pointers and German Shepherd Dogs.

Furnishing protection
Frightened by strange surroundings, this Boxer retreats under a chair, the domestic equivalent of a wolf seeking the security of the den. When approached, she might simply freeze. This is learned, rather than instinctive, behavior.

They can't reach me now.

Body is drawn back in typical cowering position

In a corner
With nowhere to hide, this German Shepherd Dog turns to aggression for security, a common trait within the breed. I sometimes encounter this behavior at the veterinary clinic. A shivering and fearful dog, with ears back and tail between its legs, feels cornered and suddenly threatens when approached.

The best defense is attack.

Eye contact is held

My Dad's bigger than you are.

Ears show worry and concern

Yawning with fright
This Whippet shows the natural physical signs of fear. He yawns, his eyes are widely dilated, and he trembles. He also signals submission by laying his ears flat, and hides behind the security of the pack leader. In extreme fear, a dog will discharge its anal glands.

Leg is lifted submissively

Tower of strength (LEFT)
Dogs feel most secure when their owners are present. They try to hide behind their legs when they are worried or feel they are in danger, just as children sometimes do. This dog is about to ask to be picked up.

A Lifetime of Learning

THROUGHOUT THEIR LIVES, dogs are constantly learning. We use this trait, training dogs to work for us in a variety of ways, from acting as eyes or ears for blind or deaf people, to guarding property and protecting us on command. Even when they are not actively trained, dogs monitor our routines and teach themselves about the world they see. With age, mental activity slows down, and the brain actually shrinks. Routine becomes more important. But even in old age, a dog's mental activities can be preserved by constantly providing stimulating activity.

Aggression to order (ABOVE)
On command, this trained guard dog attacks a mock intruder. Trained to "retrieve" villains rather than attack them, these dogs can be aggressive one moment, then gentle once the target is under control.

How about a game?

Old dog, new tricks (ABOVE)
Although he is quite old, this Golden Retriever still finds it enjoyable to play with a new and interesting object. Through constant daily exercise he retains a youthful enjoyment of life.

Double trouble (RIGHT)
This Groenendael (Belgian Shepherd Dog) looks quizzical as she catches sight of her image in the mirror. Dogs learn throughout their lives, but some things remain inexplicable.

Tail hangs limp, showing no alarm

As old as you feel (ABOVE)
*Seeing the Basenji playing with a ball,
an elderly Gordon Setter ambles over
to join in. Dogs remain curious and
sociable in old age if they have
stimulating lives.*

Do not disturb (RIGHT)
*A puppy backs away from his grandmother, who
is snarling because she is surprised by his
unexpected approach. Old dogs can get
very set in their ways and should
not be suddenly disturbed.*

*I'm irritable.
Don't bother me.*

Teeth are
displayed

Dog retracts head
in puzzlement

Head is tilted
quizzically

*I don't
understand.
Who is that?*

THE GROWING FAMILY

The soft answer
The puppy on the ground inhibits her bite, turning a fight into a game. Playing like this avoids causing serious damage, and at the same time helps to determine rank.

DOGS VARY TREMENDOUSLY, but they all share common characteristics, especially in breeding. The brief courtship and the physical linking of male and female dogs in mating are the same in the tiniest lapdog and the largest of the defense breeds. So is the behavior of the pregnant female: she becomes quieter, grows possessive of articles such as toys, prefers to stay under tables or chairs, and sometimes becomes snappy. These changes, which are motivated by hormones, also occur during false pregnancies.

At birth the mother is in control, severing the umbilical cords, drying the puppies, and helping them to find her milk. The puppies are born with very few senses, and are completely dependent upon her. But the sensory abilities develop within weeks, and with them comes independence. Soon the puppies are exploring their world, learning to manipulate both each other and any objects that they find, and demanding food as well as milk from their harassed

Topsy-turvy
These six-week-old puppies play rough-and-tumble, improving their coordination, balance, and reflexes.

Childhood games
While one puppy nonchalantly chews on the leg of another, a third puppy joins in the game. Play is a juvenile activity, accentuated by selective breeding to continue through life.

94

mother. This is the only time in the lives of most dogs that they are part of a true pack. The mother is the pack leader, but a hierarchy develops among the puppies. In their games, teamwork is learned and behavior is set for life.

Mother love
With their mother standing contentedly, these four-week-old puppies take a meal. They are dependent upon her until they reach the age when, in the wild, they could hunt for themselves.

Fight for a place
Through this kind of play-fighting, young dogs determine their future places in the developing hierarchy.

Three's a crowd?
These three-week-old puppies huddle together for security and warmth. As pack animals, they will continue to enjoy contact with others, including us, even when fully grown.

Because we control their breeding, we can accentuate or diminish the characteristics of dogs. In this way we have created the different breeds. Some dogs are easily trained, others are independent. Certain breeds thrive on companionship, while others are very territorial. Some breeds are more excitable than others. By choosing carefully, you can select a canine companion who will enhance your life and that of your family.

Choosing a Partner

ALTHOUGH IT MAY appear that the male initiates courtship, it is actually the female who decides when – and with whom – she will mate. She does not necessarily choose the most dominant male. Females prefer familiar partners and might simply roll over in submission to over-dominant dogs. While males are always sexually active, females normally have only two short spells each year when they ovulate and then willingly mate. Before and just after ovulation, bitches become more playful, soliciting interest from male dogs.

2 Role reversal
During pre-mating games, the female clasps the male from behind and mounts him. Sometimes she will also carry out pelvic thrusts. Although he is disconcerted, he does not become aggressive because of the prospect of mating.

Wait a minute, shouldn't I be doing that?

Front paws surround dog's midriff

Ears pricked forward in alert position

Front legs sink into play-bow position

1 Play-bowing
Having scented that the female is in season, the male dog confidently approaches her. She replies with a play-bow, which invites him to join in play activity while telling him that she is not yet ready to mate.

How about a game?

3 Brief interlude (RIGHT)
Standing still and with his tail wagging with excitement, the male allows the female to investigate him. She licks her nose to allow scent molecules to be caught more readily so that she can scent him better. After a short pause, play continues.

Tail raised in excitement

5 Standing ready
Once sure that the male is an acceptable mate, the female stands still. She draws her tail to the side, displaying her vulva. She only behaves like this after ovulation.

Tail drawn aside

4 Playing around
Play-wrestling is often initiated by the female. It allows her to make frequent body contact with her partner. Both dogs roll and tumble, growling all the time, while the male takes the opportunity to thrust with his pelvis.

I'm ready when you are.

Heavy panting to cool off after activity

97

Mating

AFTER all the elaborate procedures of courtship, the act of mating is completed quickly. As soon as the bitch stands for him, the dog mounts her, grasping her body with his forelegs and pushing his chest onto her back. During sexual congress, the male may sometimes gently hold on to the female with his teeth, and also lick areas of her head, especially around the ears. The male ejaculates quickly, but the two dogs remain physically locked together in a "tie" for about half an hour. This period prevents other dogs from mating with the female.

1 Standing receptively
As the female stands waiting with her tail turned to one side, the male excitedly sniffs and licks her vulva. If she resumes play, he will mark a nearby spot with urine. However, if she remains still he knows that she is ready to mate.

Dogs are physically united with each other

98

2 Check and mate (LEFT)
When the male approaches, the female turns her tail away from him. Initially he stands squarely to her side and rests his head on her back. He licks or nibbles her and, if she shows no resentment, prepares to mount.

3 Copulation (BELOW)
While the bitch stands still, often with her eyes partly closed, the male clasps her waist with his forepaws and starts making pelvic thrusts. Ejaculation starts almost immediately.

Female stands passively

Forelegs clasp female's body

4 The tie that binds (LEFT)
As mating is completed, a balloon-like apparatus at the base of the dog's penis swells up, preventing the couple from separating. He lifts up one of his hind legs to step over her, but they remain locked together in the "tie" for between five and fifty minutes.

Eyes close and dog relaxes

5 Tidying up
As soon as the dog's swelling relaxes, the pair "untie" and retire to lick their genitals. This is a simple sanitary gesture that reduces the possibility of infection. After a variable interval, they may mate once more.

Genitals are cleaned

Pregnancy Behavior

ONCE HER SEASON (or period "in heat") has finished, a female dog behaves as if she is pregnant regardless of whether she has successfully mated or not. This happens because the hormone of pregnancy (progesterone) is always produced by the body for a two-month period after ovulation. During this time a bitch tends to be quieter and more reclusive, but she may also be snappy and irritable. In addition, during her pregnancy or false pregnancy, she may become unusually possessive over any belongings, especially soft toys. You may also see her scratch and dig in carpets or earth and create "dens" around the home, often under tables or chairs.

Toy possession (RIGHT)
Finding denlike security under a chair, a female dog exhibits her hormonally influenced maternal behavior by caring for a stuffed toy, sniffing its ears, and then licking them. She behaves this way after her season, irrespective of whether she is really pregnant.

Toy is groomed

Eyes close in contentment

What a weight to lug around.

Late pregnancy
In the last stage of pregnancy, a bitch lies on her side in what is now the most comfortable position for her. The size of her swollen abdomen indicates that she is due to give birth imminently.

Occupying a real den
Few of our domestic dogs have the opportunity to do so, but this pregnant female has dug herself an underground den to which she can retreat to whelp her litter. Housebound dogs will find artificial "dens" under the furniture.

I have to find somebody to look after.

The kitten is groomed as if it is a puppy

Kittens investigate foster mother

Mothering another species
Impelled by her need to nurture, this bitch has adopted an orphan litter of kittens, which she grooms as she would her own puppies. Her behavior derives from her past experience as a mother and from progesterone, which is the hormone of pregnancy.

Tail lies relaxed

Abdomen is distended by growing puppies

Giving Birth

As BIRTH APPROACHES, the mother becomes restless and stops eating. She may be wary of strangers, or react aggressively if disturbed. In labor, the intensity of her contractions varies, and she might pant heavily or take slow, deep breaths. Puppies are delivered at intervals ranging from a few minutes to two hours in length. Some dogs even temporarily inhibit their contractions when they see their owners. Birth can be physically difficult in some modified breeds, such as Bulldogs, which may need veterinary help during delivery. If your dog experiences any birthing problems, you should contact a vet immediately.

1 Last things first
With rhythmic contractions, the mother expels a puppy in its birth sac. Most puppies emerge headfirst, in a diving position, but it is not unusual for them to enter the world tailfirst, as this one is doing. In the meantime, the puppies that have already been born huddle close to their mother for warmth.

2 Severing the ties
This experienced mother has already licked away the sac from the puppy's face, allowing it to breathe. She now turns her attention to chewing through the umbilical cord, severing the puppy from the afterbirth.

Cord is bitten through

3 Licked into shape
The mother dries her puppies with meticulous licking, and stimulates them to empty their bladders and bowels by licking the anogenital regions. These systems are already functioning but are not under the newborn puppies' control.

Anogenital regions are licked

Easy. Like peas from a pod.

4 Mother's milk
During a pause in whelping, the mother turns to check on her puppies' feeding arrangement. Inexperienced mothers do not usually feed their young until after the last delivery, but this mother is happy to let her puppies find her teats as soon as they can. She has already eaten their afterbirths.

Ear position shows her active interest

Legs stretched out for balance

Puppies immediately seek milk and warmth

Just checking that everything's OK.

5 Well-earned rest
Having successfully delivered all six puppies, licked them dry, and cleaned up as much of the mess of birth as she can to protect them from possible predators, the mother now relaxes and gives her newborn family an uninterrupted feed. If undisturbed, she will not leave her puppies for the next 24 hours.

6 Dependent offspring
Dry and with full stomachs, these one-hour-old puppies are almost totally helpless and completely dependent upon their mother for warmth, food, and protection. She will only retrieve straying puppies if they cry out, but feeds them without their asking.

Eyes and ears are closed at birth

Puppies huddle together for warmth and to feed

Raising the Family

THE MOTHERING INSTINCT is elicited immediately after birth by the appearance and erratic movement of the puppies, factors that also evoke caring instincts in us. The instinctive behavior in the mother progresses naturally from total concern for her puppies' protection, nourishment, cleanliness, and sanitation, through a stage of teaching discipline, to treating her young as other adult members of a pack when they become competition with her. This rapid evolution in maternal behavior allows the puppies to become independent of their mother by the time they are three months old.

Game for anything
By joining in their games, this mother helps her puppies to develop their coordination and reflexes. Play situations such as this often end in overt mothering activities, such as grooming.

Toilet training
The mother grooms one of her puppies and, by licking its anogenital region, stimulates it to urinate and defecate. These are body functions it cannot initially carry out without her help. To hide signs of the presence of her defenseless young she consumes their body wastes.

Puppy cowers away from mother's rough play

Puppy accepts grooming

I'd better clean him up.

Constant care (RIGHT)
While two of her puppies feed, this experienced mother licks the ear of another. Feeding and grooming are pleasurable activities for her, but both become an increasing strain as the puppies mature and become more active.

Teaching manners
Because she has been bitten too hard during play, the mother disciplines her puppy by growling and pinning him to the ground. This teaches the puppy that during play he must control the severity of his bite.

Who says you can't do two jobs at once?

Swollen teats show that mother is still lactating

Mother licks inside of puppy's ear

Puppies can now feed standing up

105

Senses of Independence

FOR THE FIRST week of life, puppies find their mother or each other through scent, touch, and the heat receptors on their noses. Their eyes and ears do not function until they are two weeks of age but are fully developed after only another two weeks. Taste and smell, present at birth, also develop rapidly over the first five weeks of life. Developing senses give the puppies greater independence: when newborn puppies are cold, they cry to attract their mother, but by three weeks of age the touch receptors on their feet have matured, and their ability to orient themselves is sophisticated enough to allow them to seek her out.

Precocious nose
A five-week-old puppy pauses in play to sniff urine scent on his littermate. Scenting ability is present at birth, and is mature by four weeks of age.

Body heat
In the absence of their mother, these one-week-old puppies huddle together for warmth.

Zzzzzz

106

Puppy licks and sniffs ear

Someone to lean on (ABOVE)
*This five-week-old puppy sniffs his
playmate's ear, balancing
himself by placing a
forepaw on her face.
Even at this age, all
of his sensory
abilities have
already matured
to adult level.*

Call of the wild
A young wolf cub cries for attention, in the
same way that dog puppies call to their
mother. At birth, wolf cubs only have the
ability to squeak and cry, just like
puppies, but within four weeks they
will growl, bark, and howl in an adult
fashion. Rapid development of the
senses and faculties is necessary
to help the young wolf scent,
see, and signal danger, as well
as to help it simply to keep
up with the pack.

Still little tail
movement at
two weeks

Present and almost correct
*Although they have been open for five days, this
two-week-old puppy's eyes are only now
becoming functional. It will be another two
weeks before her ability to see is
completely developed.*

*It's all dark
and quiet.*

Sight and sound
*Although she has
grown rapidly since
birth, this one-week-old puppy remains
deaf and sightless. In another week her
ears will open, and loud sounds will
startle her.*

Claws are
extended for
gripping

Little Beggars

URING THE FIRST three weeks of life, the mother decides when to feed her puppies. As soon as they can walk, however, they start demanding food from her. Taking the initiative, they follow her around and try to feed whenever possible – even when she is simply standing still. This behavior not only satisfies their hunger, but also provides continuing contact comfort, acting as a bonding mechanism between mother and young. As the puppies' digestive systems mature, they eat their first solid food. In wolves and feral dogs, the mother first regurgitates food for them, and then carries food to them intact.

Anything in there today?

No resentment as puppy looks for food

Milk is drying up

I actually enjoy this.

Recycled food (ABOVE)
Sticking his muzzle into his mother's mouth, this puppy tries to stimulate her to regurgitate a meal for him. Wolves introduce solid food to their cubs this way, and some dogs regurgitate in a similar fashion. This is also why dogs willingly eat food that they have just vomited up.

Hind legs splayed out for balance

108

Family provider (LEFT)
The puppies gather around their mother, pestering her for solid food. In the absence of humans, she would now be bringing back meat from hunting for them to eat.

Adapting natural behavior (RIGHT)
While his mind is still completely open to learning, this Boston Terrier puppy learns to beg for food from a human, his new "mother." He stands on his hind legs to get close to the food, just as he would do to get near his mother's mouth.

Forelegs wave to keep balance

Anything in there today?

Old habits die hard (BELOW)
Seeing their chance, these six-week-old puppies latch on for a meal. Because it is also comforting to their mother, she stops what she is doing and permits them to suckle, even though they are now old enough to do without milk.

Tail hangs relaxed

She's still everything to us.

109

Learning to Move

OVING FROM helplessness to independence depends upon the speedy development of a puppy's ability to investigate its environment. Within weeks, it must learn how to keep up with adults, to avoid predators, and to catch prey. With a nervous system that matures rapidly, a puppy can stand within two weeks of birth, walk at three weeks, and run by five weeks. Its brain is fully mature and it has all the gaits of the adult by the time it is just twelve weeks old.

Tail is used for balance

1 Three hours old (ABOVE)
At birth, this puppy can right himself if he rolls over, and can raise his head. Using heat sensors in his nose, he can also locate his mother and waddle to her for warmth and food.

Eyes are now open and focused

Paws are placed with deliberation and coordination

Wow! This is amazing.

5 Six weeks old
The puppy has developed dexterity and confidence in his movements. His reflexes are well-developed and, combined with his now mature senses, give him all that he needs to investigate the world around him.

Head can be lifted

2 One week old (BELOW)
Although he has more thrusting power in his hind legs, there has been no dramatic change in the puppy's mobility during the first seven days.

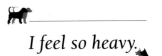

I feel so heavy.

Movement is seal-like

3 Two weeks old
Using all four legs, the puppy can now just raise himself off the ground. Improved coordination and balance allow him to take his first steps.

Legs are not yet strong enough to support body

Left...right...left...

4 Three weeks old (BELOW)
The puppy now has all the abilities to make decisions about where he wants to be, and moves in the direction of his choice.

Body is lifted off the ground

111

Exploring the World

ONCE THEIR SENSES and coordination are well developed, puppies start exploring their surroundings. In a short time, they must learn how to survive in, and benefit from, the environment around them. In addition, they must understand how to live communally with other members of their pack. At first their tremendous curiosity has no fear attached to it. They boldly leave the nest and explore the surrounding territory, willingly approaching all animals, including humans. This is a critical period in the puppies' lives: their early experiences form the backbone of lifelong behavior. Although fear behavior develops at around eight weeks of age, this period of social exploring and open learning continues for another month.

Now, that looks interesting.

1 Off to explore
Seeing two of his littermates involved in physical activity, a third puppy appears to become interested in their behavior and approaches them.

Chewing is "inhibited" and playful

I just felt something on my back – and it wasn't you.

Legs are lifted to kick playmate

Whoops! There's something in my way.

2 Overcoming obstacles
In fact, the puppy's curiosity has been stimulated by something else. Too young to have learned that he could be encountering a serious fight and putting himself at risk, the puppy determinedly takes the shortest possible route to his destination and nonchalantly climbs over the other two puppies.

Hind leg stretches to climb over obstacle

Playing puppies show no concern

Puppy gently bites playmate's neck

3 Soldiering on
Although they are being used as a jungle gym, the two littermates continue their spirited encounter. The inquisitive puppy is too interested in what he sees ahead to join in their activity and continues moving toward the focus of his attention.

4 Activity continues
As the lone puppy goes off to explore what intrigues him, his two littermates continue their play-fight (left). The minds of these puppies are like blank pages: the more they explore their surroundings and learn about each other at this age, the better prepared they will be to cope with anything new and challenging they come across in the future.

Wagging tail indicates excitement

Private Investigators

THE TIME FROM birth to three months of age is the most important in a dog's life. This is when it learns about itself, its littermates, and the world around it. It discovers what is fun and what is dangerous, and how things taste and feel. Skills are honed, and mental and physical dexterity developed by playing with objects. The more a young dog is allowed to investigate its surroundings, the more developed its brain becomes.

Is it edible?
Showing his excitement, this puppy play-bows while chewing on a toy. The chemical senses of smell and taste are the ones first used by puppies to investigate their surroundings.

Raised tail shows interest

Good muscle control has developed

I wonder if it will run away?

Puppy shows good balance

Checking it out
With her foreleg raised and extended, a puppy examines a new object by touching it. She will bat it about before tasting it.

Comfort chew (RIGHT)
Puppies seek out familiar scents. Finding a shoe that carries the scent of her owner, this Golden Retriever puppy settles down for a chew. If she is allowed to chew on an old shoe, she will go on to chew on any others with the same scent.

114

Young explorers
Two gray wolf cubs investigate a set of antlers. Young canines will investigate, play with, and manipulate any objects they find around them, such as twigs, leaves, or the remains of dead animals.

Feels good, but it doesn't taste very exciting.

Sharp teeth puncture and tear

Toy is held between paws

Sibling rivalry
Three littermates argue over who gets the prize. It seems appealing because they are fighting over a toy, but they would do the same over a recent kill.

Safe toys (LEFT)
Wool provides a chewable feel that this Border Collie puppy finds pleasurable. The best toys for puppies are those that feel good to chew but cannot be swallowed.

Chewing this shoe reminds me of my people.

Puppy is relaxed by familiar scent

115

Puppy Play

JUST LIKE US, dogs remain playful throughout their lives. This is a characteristic of their behavior that we have exaggerated through selective breeding, because we enjoy watching them play and playing with them. Dogs are most playful while they are young, and through play they learn how to communicate with each other and, most importantly, how to inhibit their bite. Play stimulates inventiveness and teaches problem-solving, timing, balance, and coordination, allowing puppies to experiment in safe conditions.

Chasing tails
Three littermates bite and chase each other. If they bite too hard, they will provoke a similar response from their playmates, so they soon learn to bite gently.

Tail is raised in excitement

Face-to-face
Growling and facing each other, these puppies gently try to bite each other's faces. This play activity continues throughout life, and is one of the most common forms of play in adults.

Turns to "attack" littermate

116

Assertiveness training
Having been bitten too hard by a larger littermate, the smaller puppy bites back, warning that it will not be intimidated. Social rank is determined in exchanges like this one.

Vulnerable abdomen is exposed

Youthful bravado
Because he has not yet developed fear behavior, this Golden Retriever puppy lies on his back and paws at the German Shepherd Dog puppy's face. Later he will adopt this position only in submission.

Head is turned in submission

Larger puppy tries to escape

Don't do that again!

Formal bow
Asking to play, this puppy lowers itself into the classic play-bow. Dogs use this stance to tell one another that they are not threatening and would simply like to meet. As an adult, this puppy will behave in the same way with humans or any other animals to which it has formed attachments.

Will you play with me?

Body is lowered to ground

Extended Family

TRUE, UNALLOYED pack behavior exists only during the brief period that a litter remains together. Once a puppy leaves its mother and siblings, it develops modified pack behavior, with humans taking the place of other canine pack members. Only puppies that go on to live or work with other dogs find themselves in a situation where they must cope on their own with the admission of new members to their group. In these circumstances, age, sex, size, and self-confidence determine where the new pack members find themselves in the canine hierarchy.

Order of seniority
When meeting an older dog for the first time, this eight-week-old puppy is put in his place by the senior dog's confident show of authority.

Dominant clasp

Mixed bag
This family group incorporates the mother, a daughter from a previous litter, and the grown puppies, each knowing its place in the pack hierarchy.

We know each other well.

Raised tail shows confidence

2 Coordinated attack (RIGHT)
Seeing what is happening, the rest of the litter joins in and threatens the stranger as a group. The puppies act as a team because they know each other very well.

3 Sexual harassment (LEFT)
A litter member mounts the intruder, showing dominance. Mounting and pelvic thrusting are basically sex-related activities, but they are also used to assert authority.

1 Not one of us (ABOVE)
Seeing a small stranger, a 12-week-old member of the pack intimidates it by dominantly placing a paw on the intruder's shoulder. The smaller outsider backs away.

We don't like strangers.

4 Standing his ground (RIGHT)
Although smaller, the intruder gains confidence and snaps back. By doing so, he proclaims that he will not be intimidated.

Family saga (BELOW)
Previous generations will continue to live with their litter, like this mother and one of her offspring. Older dogs are still members of the pack, although with advancing age they relinquish the leadership to a younger generation.

Larger puppy pulls back

Coordinated response to sound

119

Breed Characteristics

THROUGH SELECTIVE breeding, we have produced dogs with widely varying characteristics. Some are excitable, reacting quickly to their surroundings, while others are more placid. Some are more easily trained than others. Some have been bred to be aggressive guard dogs, others to be docile pets. This chart gives a guide to the levels of these traits in different breeds and, where appropriate, breed groups.

Breeds	Excitability & Activity			Aggression			Trainability		
	High	Med	Low	High	Med	Low	High	Med	Low
Afghan Hound			●		●				●
Airedale Terrier	●			●				●	
Akita			●	●			●		
Alaskan Malamute			●	●					●
American Cocker Spaniel	●				●			●	
Australian Shepherd			●			●	●		
Australian Silky Terrier	●			●				●	
Basset Hound			●			●			●
Beagle	●				●				●
Bearded Collie		●			●		●		
Bichon Frise	●				●		●		
Bloodhound			●			●			●
Boston Terrier	●				●				●
Boxer	●				●				●
Briard		●			●			●	
Brittany Spaniel			●		●		●		
Cairn Terrier	●			●				●	
Cavalier King Charles Spaniel	●					●	●		
Chesapeake Bay Retriever			●			●	●		
Chihuahua	●			●				●	
Chow Chow			●	●					●
Dachshunds	●			●					●
Dalmation			●	●					●
Doberman			●	●			●		
English Bulldog			●			●			●
English Cocker Spaniel		●			●		●		
German Shepherd Dog			●	●			●		

Breeds	Excitability & Activity			Aggression			Trainability		
	High	Med	Low	High	Med	Low	High	Med	Low
German Shorthaired Pointer			●			●	●		
Golden Retriever			●			●	●		
Great Dane			●	●					●
Hungarian Viszla			●			●	●		
Irish Setter	●				●				●
Jack Russell Terrier	●			●					●
Keeshond			●			●	●		
Labrador Retriever			●			●	●		
Lhasa Apso	●				●				●
Maltese Terrier	●				●				●
Miniature Poodle	●				●		●		
Miniature Schnauzer	●			●				●	
Newfoundland			●			●	●		
Norwegian Elkhound			●			●		●	
Old English Sheepdog			●			●			●
Pekingese	●				●				●
Pomeranian	●				●			●	
Pug	●				●				●
Pyrenean Mountain Dog			●	●				●	
Rottweiler			●	●			●		
Rough Collie			●			●	●		
Saint Bernard			●	●					●
Samoyed			●	●					●
Scottish Terrier	●			●				●	
Shetland Sheepdog	●					●	●		
Shih Tzu	●				●		●		
Siberian Husky			●	●					●
Springer Spaniels	●				●		●		
Staffordshire Bull Terrier	●				●				●
Standard Poodle			●		●		●		
Weimaraner		●			●			●	
Welsh Corgis	●			●			●		
West Highland White Terrier	●			●					●
Wirehaired Fox Terrier	●			●					●
Yorkshire Terrier	●				●			●	

Assessing your Dog's Character

EACH DOG IS AN individual with its own mind. Dogs have emotions. They feel happy, sad, jealous, angry, and exhilarated. They experience pain, humiliation, elation, and joy. Each has its own unique personality, influenced by genetics, hormones, early learning, and the environment in which a dog finds itself. Looks can sometimes be deceptive – even the most appealing-looking dog retains in some measure the traits of its wild forebears.

The hangdog
Some dogs retain the size of certain wolf breeds but have dramatically altered looks. With his low-set, lopped ears and sad eyes, this Italian Spinone looks unthreatening and easygoing. Visually he gives the impression of a sociable and relaxed personality, but looks can deceive. Some dogs that look soft, gentle, and easygoing to us might in fact be dominant individuals.

Lopped ears look
unthreatening

Large size similar to
that of wolf ancestors

The infant dog
We have created dogs that serve human emotional needs. Dogs that look and act like this Boston Terrier bring out the parent in us. Their large, prominent eyes, together with their flattened faces and small bodies, elicit a caring response from many people. However, this little dog's assertive personality can be quite at odds with the image that it projects.

Large eyes look
innocent and
trusting

Small body
appears infantile
and helpless

Your dog's personality

Many of us enjoy the company of our pet dogs so much that we tend to overlook or brush aside their misdemeanors. It is possible to assess both the positive and the negative aspects of your dog's personality using the following questionnaire. Score each group of questions separately to help you to judge exactly how trainable, domineering, sociable, or active your dog is.

If you would like to help in a worldwide study of dog behavior, please photocopy the completed questionnaire and send it to: Dr. Bruce Fogle, Box DDK, 86 York Street, London W1H 1PD, England.

Check the most appropriate box for each of the statements below.	Almost always (1)	Usually (2)	Sometimes (3)	Rarely (4)	Almost never (5)	Assess your dog's personality by adding up the scores for each section.
1. MY DOG:						**1. TRAINABILITY**
Is poor at learning obedience						A score of 12 or more means that your dog is trainable and easy to control. Excitable dogs find training difficult because they are easily distracted.
Is or was difficult to house-train						
Is excitable						
2. MY DOG:						**2. SUBMISSION**
Disobeys or even threatens me						Dogs with scores of over 20 in this section make the best family pets. If the score is less than 10, contact your veterinarian or a dog handler for professional advice.
Is dominant toward other dogs						
Barks at sudden noises at home						
Is aggressive to strangers at home						
Is snappy when disturbed						
3. MY DOG:						**3. SOCIABILITY WITH HUMANS**
Is hostile to people						Scores of over 16 show the dogs that have best integrated themselves into human society. A low score means that your pet is poorly socialized and is a potential fear-biter.
Will not accept strangers						
Dislikes being petted						
Is likely to snap at children						
4. MY DOG:						**4. SOCIABILITY WITH OTHER DOGS**
Is fearful of other unknown dogs						Dogs that have scores of 12 or more enjoy canine company. These are the animals that would most appreciate living with fellow dogs.
Is tense and nervous						
Will not play with other dogs						
5. MY DOG:						**5. ACTIVITY**
Is destructive						A score of 16 or more means that your dog is relaxed and self-contained. Dogs with low scores need extra physical and mental activity. These are inherited traits over which you have little control.
Barks when anxious or excited						
Whines/demands my attention						
Demands physical activity						

- *What is the breed of your dog?* ....
- *What color is your dog?* ....
- *How old was your dog when you acquired him/her?* ....
- *How old is your dog now?* ....
- *Is your dog male or female?* ....
  - *Has your dog been neutered?* ....
    - *If so, at what age was your dog neutered?* ....
    - *In what country do you live?* ....

TOTAL SCORE

A score of under 40 means that your companion is a potential problem dog. You should contact your veterinarian for professional advice. A total score of over 70 means that you are sharing your home with an angel.

Useful Addresses

DOG TRAINING

All breeds of dogs, regardless of their size, should be given thorough obedience training. The earlier training is started, the better the chances of success are: training should start on the day that you get your new dog, whether it is an adult or a puppy. Contact your veterinarian for advice on dog training facilities in your area.

ORGANIZATIONS

American Boarding Kennels Association
4575 Galley Road, Suite 400A
Colorado Springs, CO 80915
Holds national and regional conventions; publishes lists of kennels and experts; monthly publication.

American Kennel Club (AKC)
51 Madison Avenue
New York, NY 10010
Largest nonprofit all-breed registry; sanctioning body for over 11,000 annual events.
Publications, educational literature, audiovisual materials, largest dog library in the country, open to the public.

American Society for the Prevention of Cruelty to Animals (ASPCA)
441 East 92nd Street
New York, NY 10028
Nonprofit animal advocacy group; America's oldest humane society. Educational information, publications, audiovisual materials, legislative support and activities nationwide, behavior hotline for NYC area.

American Veterinary Medical Association
1931 North Meacham Road
Schaumburg, IL 60173
Informational brochures and career information.

Assistance Dog Institute
421 East Cotati Avenue
Cotati, CA 94931-4000
Research and development on assistance and therapy dogs.

Delta Society
P.O. Box 1080
Renton, WA 98057 1080
Pet Partners Program and Resource Center on hearing dogs.

Humane Society of the United States
2100 L Street, NW
Washington, DC 20037
Publications, specialty items, audiovisual materials, legislative and investigative activity.

PUBLICATIONS

Dog Fancy
P.O. Box 53264
Boulder, CO 80322

Dog World
29 North Wacker Drive
Chicago, IL 60606

Groom and Board
207 S. Wabash Avenue, Suite 504
Chicago, IL 60604

Purebred Dogs/American Kennel Gazette
American Kennel Club
51 Madison Avenue
New York, NY 10010

Index

Acknowledgments

Author's acknowledgments

Now that you've read the book, you'll understand how much fun it was to produce. Imagine working with the variety of dogs in these pictures! I feel more proprietorial about this book than any other. I've known David Ward, the photographer, for 12 years. He's my head nurse's husband. I know almost every dog in the book, because they're patients, and I know several especially well. Edwin, the boxer, comes to work with her owner, Amanda Topp, one of my veterinary nurses. The Italian Spinones, Badger and Hattie, also live their days at my veterinary clinic. They belong to my other nurse, Jenny Berry. And you might notice a couple of Golden Retrievers appearing here and there with their female owner. They're all mine! Thanks to all of them, and to Ashley McManus, another nurse who worked so willingly on the book.

If you think we enjoyed the photo sessions, the dogs loved them even more. We made sure that nothing unpleasant happened. All the dogs showing aggression were chosen because they would turn it on and off at their owners' commands. And for all the sequences on dominance and submission we had a superb dog handler and trainer, Colin Tennant, present.

Editorial teams can sometimes be dispassionate about assignments. Not so this team. Krystyna Mayer brought her best friend's Akita to a shoot and willingly got slobbered on. Roger Smoothy was there each week, graciously allowing dogs to fantasize that he was a fire hydrant, and Candida Ross-Macdonald whizzed in when Roger was called off to another assignment. All the while, Nigel Hazle told us about the joys of parenthood and drolly commented that we, and he, were all nuts. Thanks to all of them for their enjoyable company, and to Derek Coombes for saying "yes" whenever we asked questions.

Finally, I hope my parents enjoy showing this one, too, to their friends.

Dorling Kindersley would like to thank:

Roger Smoothy for planning and attending photographic sessions, and initial editorial work; Vanessa Hamilton for design assistance; Mary Ann Lynch for Americanization; Janos Marffy for airbrushing; Nylabone Ltd. for plastic chews and toys; The Company of Animals Ltd. for toys; Jenny Berry for help with dogs and photography, and all the owners who brought their dogs along – there are far too many to name individually, but our thanks go out to all.

Illustrations
Rowan Clifford p.12-13 wolves
Janos Marffy p.12-13 map

Photographic credits
l = left, r = right, t = top, b = bottom, c = center

All photography by David Ward except for:
Jane Burton p.22 tl, p.71 br, p.94-119; Bruce Coleman Ltd. p.12 cl, c, p.13 cb, tr, p.17 ct, p.23 br, p.45 tr, p.55 tr, p.69 tr, p.115 ct; Dave King p.115 b; Lynn Rogers p.35 br, p.39 c, p.47 br, p.51 tr, p.59 br, p.60 cb, p.75 tr, p.80 bl, p.107 tr; Steve Shott p.16 t; Jerry Young p.13 ct.

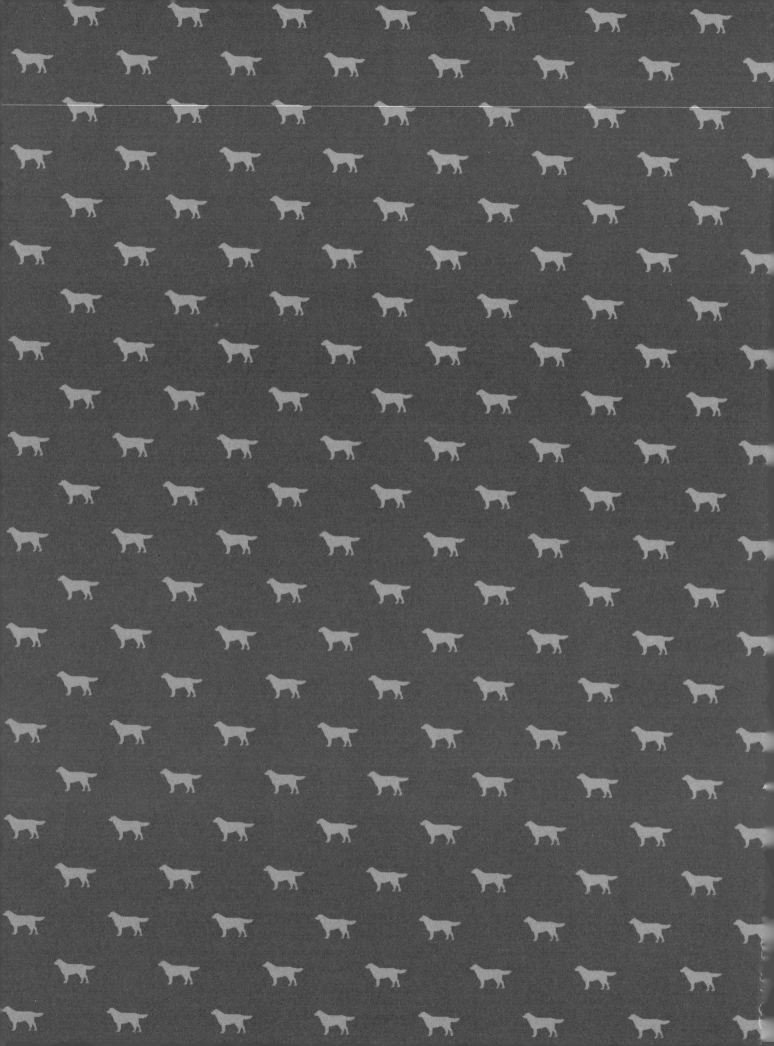